FABRICS FOR INTERIORS
A Guide for Architects, Designers, and Consumers

Jack Lenor Larsen   Jeanne Weeks

VNR VAN NOSTRAND REINHOLD COMPANY
New York Cincinnati Toronto London Melbourne

Acknowledgments

The authors express thanks to Professor Doris Brockway, for reading and correcting our text; to Olga Gueft, for her meaningful organization of the manuscript; to Henrietta Blau of Delta Upholstery, for advising us on window fabrics; and to Archie Parr, formerly of Dunbar Furniture, for his help with the upholstery section.

We thank the Larsen staff and particularly Win Anderson, for constant advice along the way; the late Professor Grace Denny, for her continuing influence in fabric technology; and Helene Margolies and Jeannette Vota, for their patience and very special assistance with unraveling the manuscript in its several manifestations.

Our thanks, too, to Tom O'Connor Sloane III of Doubleday, for his encouragement and for releasing to us a number of drawings from *Elements of Weaving* by Azalea Thorpe and Jack Larsen; to Winston Sutter of Isabel Scott Fabrics, for his advice on shading coefficients; to Joel T. Loeb and Richard R. Hess of Kiesling-Hess Finishing Company, Inc., for their instruction on finishes; and to Charles J. Kleissler and George Krunholtz of U.S. Testing Company, Inc., for their help with testing.

ISBN 0-442-24683-8 (cloth)
ISBN 0-442-24684-6 (paper)

Designed by Loudan Enterprises

Published in 1975 by Van Nostrand Reinhold Company
A Division of Litton Educational Publishing, Inc.
135 West 50th Street
New York, N.Y. 10020

Van Nostrand Reinhold Limited
1410 Birchmount Road
Scarborough, Ontario M1P 2E7, Canada

Van Nostrand Reinhold Australia Pty. Ltd.
17 Queen Street
Mitcham, Victoria 3132, Australia

Van Nostrand Reinhold Company Ltd.
Molly Millars Lane
Wokingham, Berkshire, England

16 15 14 13 12 11 10 9 8 7 6 5

Library of Congress Cataloging in Publication Data

Larsen, Jack Lenor.
  Fabrics for interiors.

  Bibliography: p.
  1. Textile fabrics.   2. Interior decoration.
I. Weeks, Jeanne G., joint author.   II. Title.
TS1767 L37   746.9   75-9117
ISBN 0-442-24683-8
ISBN 0-442-24684-6 pbk.

CONTENTS

INTRODUCTION

The purpose of this book is to make fabric selection easier and wiser, not only in terms of guiding the reader away from pitfalls and toward uses of current technology but also making him aware of what fabric is in its broadest sense.

Understanding how to choose and specify a fabric wisely gives the decorator a head start in the overall design of any room. Of course, questions of aesthetics, performance, and cost must be answered in terms of the intended function of each fabric within the room. However, that function must itself be comprehended as primarily aesthetic and psychic: that it is to make people feel more secure, more related, and more alive gives us a whole new understanding of the need for fabric. Doggedly continuing to think only in terms of windows needing curtains, and sofas covers is essentially misleading.

Perhaps it is one of evolution's little jokes that today's interiors need fabrics more desperately than did primordial caves. Despite the felicities of running water and climate control, the glass-walled shoebox cubicles of modern construction provide only undifferentiated, bare-bones shelter.

The nineteenth-century house, for all of its mechanistic naiveté, had less need for the acoustical, light-controlling, and humanizing treatments so necessary today. Its walls were thick to muffle noise; its narrow, often tall windows blocked out glare. Elaboration through architectural moldings, panelings, cornices, and parquet floors gave warmth and character, if not emphatic style, to its rooms long before they were furnished. Construction materials were overtly expressed, as were their joinings and structure. In an era of custom building, alienating anonymity was less frequent.

Today, in most instances it is not interior architecture but furnishings which must differentiate interior spaces and give them a sense of materials and of identity. Of all the furnishings available, fabric best fulfills its role as a major contributor. In application fabrics are versatile, easily handled, and economical. Because of their staggering variety and adaptability, fabrics are the most useful of props.

The purpose of this book, therefore, is to clarify just these aesthetic, functional, and technical facts which must be at the fingertips of anyone who wants to use fabrics to their best advantage.

In Part 1 the aesthetic factors are discussed; Part 2 deals with performance; Part 3 describes the physical properties of many types of fabric; Part 4, coloring; Part 5, the Market—including costs, budgeting, and investment; and Part 6 is a glossary-index of fabric terms.

5

PART 1: AESTHETICS

1-1. All things have texture, but none so inherently and with such variety as fabric. In *Cashel*, a heavy upholstery of Irish worsted, the scale of the texture is varied by the flame yarn shown in figure 3-8.

1. Texture

CHARACTERISTICS OF TEXTURE

The essential and distinguishing characteristic of fabric—what makes it a desirable material to have around us—is *texture*. Although the word itself comes from the Latin *textere*, "to weave," all fabrics—not only wovens—have texture. We are inclined to think of texture narrowly as rough or coarse-grained, but this is misleading, since sleek satins and frosty taffetas have texture also.

The essence of fabric texture is the bas-relief of highlight and shadow on the hills and valleys of the construction. Fabric texture is determined by the weave and density, the fiber content, and the manner in which the yarn is spun. Whether it is fine or coarse, mat or shiny, dry or glistening, what is important is the quality of the cumulative fiber surface.

Spinning conditions fabric texture. Silk, for instance, which is naturally lustrous and smooth, becomes pebbly and mat when it is tightly twisted into a crepe yarn. Spinning also determines whether the yarn will be fine or coarse, regular or random in profile. Loosely spun, unplied yarns in an unfinished, open-set cloth have more texture than tightly spun yarns in a finished, closely set cloth (see Part 3, section 3).

In determining texture, fabric construction—or weave—is second only to spinning. For example, the very different textures of cheesecloth, waffle piqué, velvet, and terrycloth may be woven with the same cotton yarn. The surface differences are a result of the construction. The vast differences between canvas and cheesecloth—both plain weaves—is produced solely by the *set*, or density, of the weave. One is an extremely close-set weave; the other, very open in set. *Construction*, then, as it applies to texture, is the result of the yarn, the order of interlacing, and the density (or set).

1-2. Translucency is another kind of texture and a very beautiful one. Light filtering through fibers such as this luminous Greenland wool woven through with acetate film creates a spectacular beauty akin to light passing through water. Casement designed by Paula Trock.

OPACITY AND TRANSPARENCY

As mentioned above, texture is usually thought of in terms of how rough or smooth the surface or how dull or bright the fabric is. But texture also relates to the relative opacity or transparency of the cloth and to the quality of that opacity or transparency. Fabrics can be only slightly light-admitting (*opaque*), like canvas, or so sheer (*transparent*) as to barely diffuse strong light. The many gradations between and combinations of these light-controlling extremes create innumerable possibilities for surface texture and character.

Fibers such as mohair have in themselves a crystalline translucency. When these fibers are struck by light, the whole fabric surface becomes a glowing, diffusing element. Fibers such as opaque metallics or translucent monofilaments sparkle or glisten in light. These characteristics are all textural considerations, all potential decorative devices.

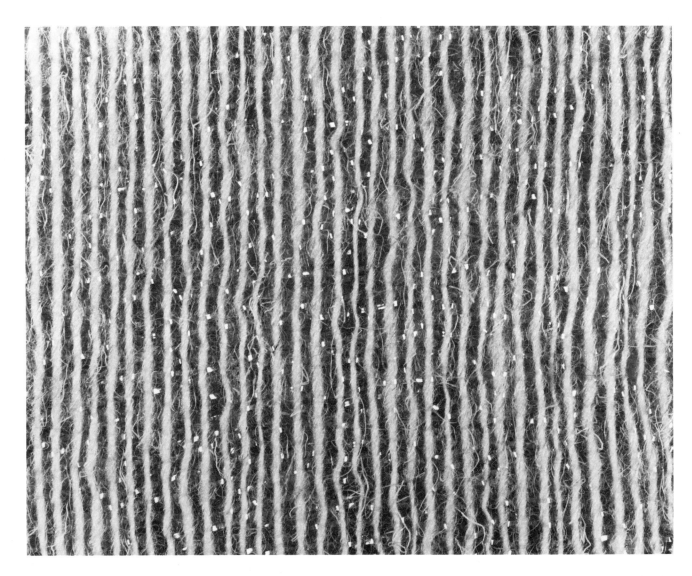

RELIEF

Visually, *relief* is read as highlight and shadow. Light direction is important, which is why we need more texture in rooms with directionless light. To the hand, texture is a broken or uneven surface. Such corrugated fabrics as corduroy and Bedford cord have a broken surface, but one which is regular and smooth. Other cloths with pronounced relief are bumpy tweeds, jagged chevrons, furry piles, or scalloped matelassés.

What the eye reads as relief may in fact be only visual: such cloths as salt-and-pepper tweeds and glen plaids may be polished and smooth to the touch; the effect of a low relief results from the eye "reading" the repeat of dark and light yarns as highlight and shadow. The texture may even be printed on the fabric (see Part 1, section 2).

1-3. Often it is not the material itself but its highlights and shadows that we read as texture. The other lesson here is a material that ages beautifully.

PSYCHIC RELIEF

The history of fabrics could be written in terms of psychic compensation. In the rural environment of the past—when houses were isolated, and entertainment infrequent—busy patterns provided stimulus. Since most people battled with the elements, they *wanted* houses that were protective and cozy. Man-made rhythms, neat and monotonous, were welcome and reassuring.

Today's urban environment is quite the opposite. Neighbors are too close; visual and aural stimulation follow us along the streets from home to job. Now a desirable place to live and work is one blessed with quiet and serenity, and urban man's idealized environment is perhaps a deserted beach with the repose of long horizontal lines, friendly light, and a soft variety of surface textures.

Ironically, the casual variety of natural textures found in sand and foliage or in hand-hewn building materials is increasingly absent from the concrete jungle of urban environment. The brash, monotonous, or slick surfaces with which man has replaced the textures of field and forest are without relief. Interiors, especially, are encased with an unrelieved smoothness of paint, plastic, and glass. *Of the materials readily available, textured fabrics most effortlessly substitute the broken color and random shade-and-shadow of nature.* The chaotic din and incessant clangor of our cities make the human psyche cry out for repose. The softness and textured surface of interior fabrics offer relief.

To compensate for overcrowding, we hunger for a sense of privacy and protection from probing eyes. At the same time we treasure a view or at least some illusion of a distant horizon. Light, airy casement fabrics provide privacy without sacrificing "borrowed" outdoor spaces or sunlight.

1-4. In nature texture changes seasonally and—with shifting light—hourly. Indoors, fabrics can do both.

2. Color

FABRIC AND COLOR

Fabric is one of the principal devices for introducing color into interiors and certainly the most easily manipulated one. Moreover, the full-color palette offered today was unobtainable in previous times. Fine differences in tone and hue are available in a range that covers the entire spectrum, and—in theory—almost all of them can be made sufficiently sunfast to meet reasonable standards (see Part 4, section 2).

Our freedom in the use of color has broadened with progress in protective finishes, which, while not entirely foolproof, have greatly reduced the hazards of unsightly soiling and staining. Light- and delicate-colored fabrics, once ruled out of most situations, can now be used more safely. (Specifics of protective finishes are given in Part 3, section 5.)

Color offers enormous decorative potential—which has hardly been explored. We are, in fact, only beginning to think in terms of interior color as an element of change comparable to turning on recorded music or to placing seasonal flowers in a room. Because fabric is easy to store and to rotate, it is an obvious vehicle for changing color. Because of fabric's relatively low cost in comparison to carpeting and furniture, such seasonal changes as slipcovers are familiar. The possibility of changing walls and windows as well—for the season or for special occasions—through the manipulation of fabric on tracks or blinds has hardly been considered outside of the theater. In truth, it is quite feasible.

NATURAL COLOR

Natural color is not flat and dull like paint but fragmented, or *broken*. Such familiar surfaces as foliage, flowers, bark, stone, or sand effuse a lively vibrancy in which minute particles of color are juxtaposed to sparkle like a galaxy in microcosm. This is *living color*, at once stimulating and soothing to weary eyes. Whether in a bird's wing or an artist's streaked paint, broken color is a visual high point.

While natural building materials such as wood or stone possess broken color, fabric is the most readily available and the least expensive means of creating this effect. *Of all man-made materials, fabric has the most—and best—potential for fracturing color.* Color breakup in fabric may be achieved in a variety of ways. The most common is by using warp yarns of one color and weft yarns of another. Other random color effects are achieved in striae, ombrés, and small-scaled checks. When the color breakup is finely scaled and close in value, the result is *iridescence*—a scintillating vibration of one color in relation to the others.

COLOR AND TEXTURE

Color judgments are in part subjective, determined by arbitrary tastes, preferences, and fashions. Of course, the major determinant in color judgment is the amount used and its juxtaposition to other colors. When anyone—including an artist or designer—tells us that a color is "good," he may simply mean that the color is one he happens to like. But his color judgments may also be selective and related to a combination of color and texture. When he speaks of good color in a mat-finished felt, he means something quite different from good color in a watered silk.

1-5. The random ribbed relief of this Berber wool upholstery is accentuated by the dark yarns, which read as deep shadow.

COLOR AND LIGHT

The selection of fabric color is complicated by our present wealth of resources. We have access to many fabrics that are appropriate to other periods and regions. Just as fabrics colored for the sparse, slanting sunlight of northern lands do not look the same in the blazing sun of the tropics, fabrics intended for regions mantled in mist have a totally different appearance where bright light and deep shadows are boldly defined. Colors designed for the age of candlelight may be disappointing in the bright glow of incandescent light or vulgar in a cold fluorescent glare.

Perhaps more dangerous is the often necessary practice of selecting in one climatic zone a fabric color that will be used in another. Thus, colors that seem "right" in the light of New York City are apt to be heavy as lead in the Caribbean—or thin and superficial in Anchorage. Try to finalize color on the spot—before orders are firm.

Color is the first and last consideration in the purchase of any fabric. In making the final fabric selection, the best solution is to judge the color within the space where it is to be used. Further, the relative colors of various fabric samples should be observed in morning, afternoon, and evening light. If the fabric is to be added to an already furnished room, its color will be relative to both light and the other colors. If samples are not available, it may well be worth the effort and even the expense of purchasing trial yardage.

In a new installation, the safest and surest, although the slowest, procedure is to develop fabric color in stages—after wall and floor colors are set and after lighting and window-shading controls are completed. Making the right choice from fabric samples at this stage is relatively simple. For the many instances in which this is not feasible, experience and a few guidelines are helpful.

Reflected Light

Undraped glass walls offer no protection from direct sunlight. Large quantities of light, even if indirect, will drench the color out of room surfaces, making them appear washed-out. Because pale interior surfaces are reflectant, they increase rather than reduce this effect.

It becomes obvious that the color and color values surrounding the space are of paramount influence. Walls, ceilings, and floors affect the manner in which the room is viewed. Not only do warm, light colors reflect more light than darker or colder tones, but their reflectant surfaces condition all other colors. Strong downlight on a red carpet, which will turn neutral walls pink, may be desirable in a restaurant or theater but not in a bank.

Artificial Light

It is reassuring to know that fabric samples of various colors that relate to each other in one light will, if allowance is made for their divergent color values, bear the same relationship in another kind of light. The major exception to this comfortable rule of thumb is the yellow-blue relationship under fluorescent light. Here, the yellow tones may become strident. Colors containing blue, such as a blue-red, may blacken under fluorescence. Because turned-down light becomes yellower, dimming systems not only reduce color but change color relationships.

A relatively new lighting system is the luminous ceiling—a light source radiating an artificially even, directionless, and shadowless glare. Under this type of light color intensities tend to be leveled, and textures washed out. To prevent bland monotony of color or texture, contrasts and intensities must be exaggerated, directional light sources added, or both.

3. Pattern

FABRIC PATTERN AS A DESIGN ELEMENT

Pattern as a design element is, of course, a subject in itself. But because fabric is undoubtedly the most flexible medium for introducing pattern within any room, a discussion of the subject is more than warranted here.

Pattern—whether integral or applied, geometric or figurative—is the visual configuration of a cloth; it is not a "design" on cloth. *Design* is the cloth in *all* its aspects, including the pattern if there is one. A *pattern repeat*, which may be half an inch or a whole wall, is one total unit. A *motif* is a pattern unit, which may be—like a chevron or polka dot—repeated over and over again or one part or aspect of a complex pattern.

Pattern enriches an area, gives variety to surfaces, fills spaces, breaks them up, orchestrates a color scheme, and can establish a directional line or movement. Pattern is the common expedient in large, insipid, or blank spaces such as institutional cafeterias, new houses, and briefly used common spaces—hallways, foyers, or powder rooms—which, more often than not, are devoid of furniture.

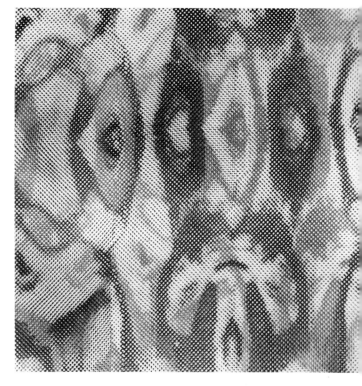

1-6. A smooth satin of Irish worsted is given texture and broken color through the vibrant effect of a pointillist printing technique, in which tiny cumulative particles of color are arranged in an ombré pattern. Designed by Nathan Shapira and Larsen Design Studio.

If a rule need be drawn, the amount of pattern should be in inverse proportion to the amount of furniture and other space-filling or space-cluttering contents of a room. At best, the scale of the pattern relates the size of the space to the scale of its contents. A relatively blank and episodically used space such as a corridor could profit handsomely from the excitement provided by a really emphatic pattern placed at the end of the vista.

Offices, with their own physioenergetic patterns, tend to need less pattern and busyness in fabric. Pattern here is best rendered in great sweeps on a super scale to triumph over the jungle of machines and conversations. Such spaces as living rooms, which are used often or for a variety of functions including quiet hours, tend to need less pattern or only soft-edge, low-contrast pattern. Similarly, the relationship between works of art and other patterns in a room is a delicate one. Banishing all pattern from such spaces is not the only solution. Structured surfaces such as parquet may be supportive; so, too, may self-toned damasks or patterns in low relief.

People often fail to realize that, visually speaking, certain things within an interior are analogous to and interchangeable with pattern. A wall of books, the vista into an adjacent room provided by an open floor plan, an outside view of gardens or skyline, a mural or other works of art are visual incidents. Where there are few such incidents, the eye needs other visual centers of gravity to focus on—places that offer some escape or release from monotony. Such releases may be provided either by an overall fabric pattern or by areas of pattern.

The psychological demand for pattern is less prevalent in modern houses dominated by the open plan and the window wall. Here, the occupant is not shut in: glimpses into adjacent rooms and landscaped vistas offer escape from enclosing walls and relief from monotony. The Victorian house was provided with a rich repertoire of architectural embellishments. But today only the avant-garde house customized by the "name" architect for a wealthy client offers, without embellishment, a varied parade of visual experiences. The average apartment or detached suburban dwelling is so barren and featureless that it can literally drive its occupants up the walls unless those walls are redeemed by visual enrichment of one form or another. Patterned or textured fabrics remain as available as ever.

STRIPES

Of all fabric patterns stripes are the most universal and the most far-ranging in character. Because weaving and most other fabric structures are composed of horizontal and vertical elements, a simple change of color, yarn, interlacing, or density will produce a stripe, often without extra effort or production cost. Checks and plaids derived from crossings of horizontal and vertical stripes multiply the possibilities—for designers of both fabrics and interior space.

Stripes may be bold or staccato, casual or symmetrically formal, as multicolored as Joseph's coat or tone-on-tone. The latter are often engineered through a change in construction—yarn size or density—such as the skip-dent and omit stripes shown in figures 3-20 and 3-21. Striping is often combined with other patterning techniques, as in striped brocades. Stripes are also found in knitted and printed fabrics. The need for stripes is universal. Perhaps their most important function is as an intermediary between plain fabrics, which generally predominate, and bold patterns used as relief or focus within a total scheme.

Matching stripes is problematic, particularly horizontal stripes in long widths of drapery or wall covering (see Part 2, section 3). On the other hand, the imaginative joining of stripes offers unique opportunities for devising larger custom patterns. For instance, mitering stripes at a right angle adds adventurous design possibilities for the rectangular surfaces of benches, pillows, or bedspreads.

To produce checkered effects, stripe joinings may be off-set. Striped panels may also be alternated with stripes in a different scale or with solid-colored panels. Or a mural scale may be created by alternating full widths of two or more colors. Full-width stripes such as the Irish wool in figure C-11 may alternately invert or "book-match" to double the repeat.

DOBBY AND JACQUARD PATTERNS

Both dobby and jacquard patterns are outgrowths of basic cloth constructions or combinations of cloth structures. The *dobby* pattern is small in scale and usually allover in type. It includes such weaves as huckaback, waffle, diaper, and double cloths. Dobby patterns are produced on a multiple-harness loom with a simple dobby attachment.

Jacquard patterns—almost unlimited in variety and complexity—are produced by the jacquard attachment—a versatile invention that allows a complete range of intricacy, scale, pattern, and repeat. It should be understood that jacquard is not a weave. It is a pattern-making attachment that can be affixed to any loom or knitting machine. It makes possible machine weaving of weaves and patterns once available only by the most painstaking and costly hand weaving on a draw loom. The jacquard attachment can also simulate the effect of embroidery and tapestry, but the more familiar jacquard cloths are brocades, brocatelles, damasks, matelassés, nottingham laces, and schiffli embroideries.

PRINTED PATTERNS

Because textile printing is a postproduction or *conversion* process, it offers the easiest and most versatile means of applying pattern. The range of both effects and costs is extremely varied. (The methods and processes of printing are described in Part 4, section 2.)

In any given period and for any given market, the variety of printed patterns far outnumbers that of woven patterns. Because of their brief start-up time and the relatively low investment required for custom orders and small yardages, printed patterns respond to fashion changes far more rapidly than woven patterns. Custom printing, which may mean either custom color or custom pattern, is a special service available with varying minimums and lead times from many houses. Large patterns are far more easily achieved by printing than by any other process.

1-7. *Hills of Home.* This printed pattern provides an illusion of space and a sense of pastoral tranquility. The easy horizontal movement is quieting. The print mixes color effectively and directly. The open areas are large enough not to compete with the slubby hand-woven silk. (Photo by Tom Crane.)

PART 2: FABRICS IN USE

2-1. A grill-like mesh of nottingham lace softens the hard lines of a city view and at the same time "borrows" space from out of doors. The cloth is Larsen Lace; interior by Larry Peabody. (Photo by Louis Reens.)

1. At the Window

FUNCTIONS OF WINDOW FABRIC

The glass walls of contemporary architecture have placed new requirements on fabrics, particularly light-diffusing ones. In our crowded cities and towns even the conventional window or opening punched in the wall requires more protection than in the past. In both cases the window needs some shield for privacy, light and glare control, insulation, and protection of interior furnishings against sun fading.

The forms of protection are many: adjustable louvers, sliding panels, blinds, or several planes of flat or draped fabric. These shielding devices— all simple solutions—can be used individually or in combination as circumstances dictate. In addition to comfort, they provide major contributions to the environmental aesthetic.

View Control

Any window treatment must consider the view. Revealing the outward view, particularly if it is beautiful, may require almost no treatment at all—not by day in any case. By night, however, unless a lighted panorama replaces the daylight scene, even the most beautiful view may turn into a black void. Cheerful night views are very rare, unfortu-

nately, but even if you have one, shielding the window for the sake of privacy may be a necessity.

Light Control

Daylight, whether it is adequate, too strong, or too weak, is controlled at the window or window wall. During the day light changes in quality and shifts in direction. At some time of the day, whatever the exposure, there is some probability of glare. To a much larger extent than is generally realized, *glare*—aggressively dominating directional light—offends the psyche, wearies body and mind, and shortens tempers. Sharpened by the high contrast of its own shadows, glare also destroys interior composition, especially color balance.

In general, a light-filtering mesh or sheer casement will reduce a slight glare sufficiently for the occupant to comfortably face the window. This filter will still allow some natural light to permeate the room. But simply filtering glare is usually not enough: in most circumstances window treatments must also admit light, exclude light, and possibly even color light.

If filtering glare and admitting light require a sheer fabric, subduing light requires a dense one. Because two layers of fabric are usually mandatory, the combination of a sheer casement and an opaque drapery is the typical solution. The layers are more manageable if they are mounted on separate tracks.

Color Value

The color value of window fabrics is as crucial as the degree of opacity and the scale of mesh. With sheer fabrics a dark value will reduce glare and—in an open mesh—increase visibility. On tower floors or windows facing water, sand, or snow, a glare-deterring dark mesh may be especially desirable. In the gray light of a city canyon a crisp, sparkling white may be a realistic choice.

As one of the functions of window fabric is to make a visual transition from dark, solid walls to light-filled voids, opaque window fabrics tend to perform best in light to middle values. Colored sheers lend their tints to the interior. In places where skies are too often gray or white rather than blue, illusions of sunlight may be suggested by yellow, gold, cream, or orange casements, which tinge the light as it passes through. Psychological relief from the chill of a long winter may be achieved by the warm tints of light as it passes through red, rose, or flame-colored casements. If the relentless white heat of summer sears the countryside, pale blue or green casements will give interiors a cooler cast, while cold or acid colors engender the unhappy sensation of being underwater.

The fineness of the casement mesh also affects the intensity of color. A diaphanous sheer of translucent yarn will color the light far more than the silhouette of a grill-like mesh.

Thermal Insulation

Even with Thermopane or double glazing, windows, particularly window walls, transmit heat and cold more rapidly than solid walls. A layer of fabric at the window slows both the loss of interior heat in cold weather and the invasion of outdoor heat in summer, cutting heating and air-conditioning bills significantly.

Direct sunlight is radiant heat: to the extent that it penetrates the room, it heats everything it falls upon. Although the best solution is to keep summer sun off the glass in the first place—from the exterior—even a sheer fabric will help to break up the sun's rays. Heavy, lined drapery with an interlining of fiber batting or lambswool will exclude heat, cold, and *sound* to an amazing degree.

Shading Coefficients

Large areas of glass create the specific problem of light and glare. But, more bothersome, they allow too much summer heat and winter cold to enter—despite recent advances in curbing the problem with double panes. Colored or tinted glass helps to a limited degree. These glasses vary both in thickness and in gradations of color—pale gray to solar bronze to the newest, mirror-surfaced glass. Ultimately the problem remains one of proper screening—usually with a casement fabric which not only filters light transmission but absorbs or reflects heat and cold.

Any casement fabric can be tested to establish its *shading coefficient*, a numerical rating that measures light transmission in relation to temperature flow. Once the number is established for a given fabric, it becomes a guideline for the architect and air-conditioning engineer, whose heating and—especially—cooling problems must be resolved during the initial planning of the space or building.

Fabric is tested in relation to a quarter-inch-thick plain plate glass with a normal rate of .78 solar transmission and to a quarter-inch-thick solar-bronze glass (the most widely used) with a normal .53 solar transmission. A semiopaque fabric of medium density could register as low as .54 behind plate glass and .47 behind solar-bronze glass. The lower the coefficient, the more effective the fabric.

Fabric houses may be able to supply the shading coefficient of some of their fabrics. Otherwise, a coefficient reading may be ordered from Matrix, Inc., 537 South 31st Street, Masa, Arizona 85204. Along with a purchase order to this firm, send a twenty-four-inch-square piece of fabric. Reply time is two weeks from receipt of fabric. The cost is approximately 75 dollars per test.

Acoustical Insulation

Just as interior fabric absorbs sounds reflected from hard surfaces, fabric at the window softens sounds created within the room and definitely helps muffle noise. If external sounds such as the clamor of traffic are a problem, lining—especially interlining—is invaluable. The slightly increased cost is compensated for by the longer life expectancy of the drapery.

To absorb indoor sounds, one of the best materials available is a spongy, fibrous drapery—one with lofty yarns separated by noticeable air spaces, such as the cutwork in figure 3-29. Not incidentally, this type of casement may be more effective and less expensive than such architectural solutions as acoustical ceilings.

Camouflage

Lighter window fabrics offer limitless opportunity for architectural correction, camouflage, and unification. Irregular or poorly proportioned windows can be masked, lengthened, or widened with light fabric—without blocking light. Such interior clutter as beams, radiators, air conditioners, or other mechanical equipment can be screened by fabrics—at will and at once. Fabric solutions are less arduous, less expensive, and often less phony than structural alteration—and they are reversible.

PERFORMANCE

Before discussing specific performance requisites, it is important to remember that attempts to establish safe rules of thumb are unrealistic. Fabric performance is relative to exposure and climate, fabrication, and especially to levels of maintenance and abuse. While the authors do not suggest throwing caution to the wind, we do maintain that a safe solution is not always the best solution. Selecting fabrics with institutional performance characteristics for a residence may be as questionable as the reverse. We have already seen that the prime requisite of decorative fabric is that it contribute toward making environmental spaces alive and particular.

We suggest a happy balance between aesthetic, personal, and practical considerations. Large, low-maintenance installations require such precautions as hanging and cleaning tests. Personal rooms and ceremonial spaces may imply very special, even innovative solutions.

Dimensional Stability

Dimensional stability, or shape retention, is a prime requirement for any fabric that hangs freely. The most noticeable changes in length result from sagging, shrinking, or hiking (alternate sagging and shrinking) in response to humidity changes.

Sagging, or elongation, is common with all fabrics, but for most the degree is slight—a tolerable two percent. Over a period of time, however, some fabrics may lengthen five percent or more. For an average hundred-inch drapery panel, this represents five inches. Heavy, loosely constructed fabrics are more prone to sagging than tightly woven ones. The weight of the fabric is another factor, particularly the weight of the horizontal filling yarns in relation to the warp: with everything else equal, a balanced cloth or one with a heavier warp than filling will be more stable. Unless they are constructed of yarns that can be effectively heat-set, knits and laces tend to sag more than weaves.

Although *shrinking* is more likely to result from washing than dry cleaning, either may cause sufficient shortening to be a major nuisance. Most fabrics available today, particularly cottons, are preshrunk. Heat-set or hydrophobic fibers such as fiberglass and polyester are usually inherently resistant to shrinkage. Oddly enough, expensive fabrics are usually not preshrunk: dry cleaning is either specified or anticipated, and the cloth is often too specialized for the testing and finishing procedures of the retail market.

2-2. *Interplay*. This dark warp-knit casement not only kills glare but silhouettes the view beyond. The slit-film yarn is soil-resistant. A closeup view is shown in figure 3-36.

Some cottons and linens, especially plain white ones, are better washed than dry-cleaned; moreover, in some locations, such as beach or mountain homes, machine washing may be more available than dry cleaning. To successfully wash window fabrics—particularly open-meshed ones—the panels must not be so large that the wet weight is unmanageable. Fabrics that are not completely preshrunk should be washed *before* makeup. Do a test piece *first*.

Shrinking also occurs if the interior atmosphere is subjected to marked changes in humidity—natural or artificial. For example, air conditioners set too quickly at a level of "high cool" can produce instant shrinking or crawling.

Hydrophilic (moisture-absorbing) changes in fabric length are caused by the fibers swelling with increasing humidity—which produces shrinking—then compressing or sagging as the humidity lowers. This alternate raising and lowering—often called *hiking* or *yoyo*—can happen within a season, sometimes within a single day. The fault is common to all weights of fabric and to most fibers, whether natural or man-made. The exceptions are *hydrophobic* (non-moisture-absorbing) fibers such as fiberglass and some synthetic filaments.

A fabric constructed with a fine warp and a heavy filling is extremely susceptible to every variation of dimensional instability. Thorough on-location testing is strongly recommended before choosing any fabric with this type of construction. For major installations it is advisable to test the performance of any fabric under the atmospheric conditions in which it is to be used. Testing is crucial in humid or variable climates.

Sound workroom practice for luxury fabrics allows for a six-inch double hem—to weight the fabric and to ensure it against calamitous shrinking. Draperies are hung out, on the site or at the workroom, for up to two weeks before the baste hem is made. Minor adjustments are made by raising or lowering drapery pins on a wide heading. Unless it is required by radical changes in length, the final hem is not made until after the first cleaning. In most instances the fabric will then be stable. Budgeting for such treatment is good business practice.

Sun Rot

Sun rot is the disintegration of fabric in sunlight. As window fabric is subjected to up to three-hundred-degree temperatures, which build up between the fabric and glass exposed to the sun, resistance to sun rot is a prime requirement. Light alone is destructive, and reflected sunlight may do as much damage as direct sun. As there is no cure for damage inflicted by light, you can only try to prevent it.

The problem is treacherous because damage is not discernible until the fabric has been destroyed. More often than not the destruction only becomes noticeable in cleaning. Either the fabric comes back from the cleaner in shreds or the cleaner, realizing the extent of the damage, refuses to process it.

With the exception of mineral fibers, all fibers are subject to sun rot. Silk, sheer cotton, and most rayons and nylons are highly susceptible. Acrylics, polyester, linen, and acetate are superior in their resistance. But the fiber alone is not the criterion. The weight and balance of the cloth and the size of the yarn—particularly in the warp—affect the degree of resistance.

It is natural to assume that a "strong" fabric is strong against all forces that may threaten it. In fact, the strongest fabric may be helplessly weak in light. To cite specific mishaps, window shades of an industrial nylon with exceptional tensile strength and abrasion resistance disintegrated after six months of exposure to north light in a New York City apartment. After nine months in Philip Johnson's famous glass house, a much touted transportation cloth—of rayon—literally fell off the furniture.

Common sense dictates protective measures in exposed areas. Drapery linings do protect the fabric they line—from fading and from disintegrating. Linings provide a uniform external appearance and improve the draping quality. With a lined fabric the only vulnerable surface is the part turned back. If an extra length (or lengths) of the fabric is purchased with the original order, it can be used for replacing light-damaged sections. For costly fabrics an interlining is a sound investment.

In a western or southern exposure most casements should never be used without such protection as blinds, shades, or blackout curtains.

Slip Resistance

Although slippage is usually not so disastrous to window fabrics as it is to upholstery, slip resistance is essential for casements. The problem is identified by the warp yarns slipping against the filling. This friction causes distortion, weakening of the fabric, and sometimes snagging. An open or loosely constructed cloth benefits from a leno, knotted, knit, or nottingham-lace construction—techniques that offer resistance to slippage.

Veil-like, translucent casement cloths that are constructed of fine or translucent yarns woven by conventional methods are less subject to slippage than are open, loosely constructed woven cloths. An open weave may be ameliorated by using fuzzy or rough yarns, which are inherently slip-resistant.

In any case fabrics are easily tested for slip resistance: if the warp and filling yarns do not "hold" together or return to some reasonable configuration when gently pulled apart, chances are that the fabric will be subject to slippage during normal use.

We cannot emphasize enough how important slip resistance is in specifying casement fabrics for public areas. It is inevitable, though unfortunate, that people tend to examine fabrics to see if they can destroy them.

Mildew, Fungus, and Insects

Resistance to mildew, fungus, and insect attack is essential. This can be secured by selecting fibers wisely and by using special finishes (see Part 3, section 5). Mildew and fungus are mainly problems in the subtropics, where heat combined with excessive humidity sponsors their growth. Although fabrics made of hydrophobic fibers tend to resist mildew, collected atmospheric soil may attract it. Both cellulosic and protein fibers are subject to mildew and molds. Both can be protected by permanent antibacterial protective finishes, applied before or after the drapery is made up.

Because they lower the fiber's ability to absorb moisture, silicone and fluorochemical finishes also tend to discourage mildew and mold.

Although air circulation and light tend to discourage moths and weevils, wool and wool-blend casements should be durably mothproofed before installation. This is usually done during the fabric-manufacturing stage. If the label does not state that a fabric is mothproof, an inquiry should be made.

Flame Retardance and Flame Resistance

Flame retardance and flame resistance in various degrees are desirable for safety's sake. In public areas and institutions these characteristics are usually required by law, which in some cases is municipal, and in others statewide. The CCT-T-191B (4903,5906) federal specifications are the foundation on which most flammability tests are based. These federal specifications do not state what results are required in various cities and states around the country but merely give a testing result. The results are based on the amount of time the fabric remains on fire or remains in a red-glow state—both measured in intervals of seconds. The size of the charred area around the point of flame contact is measured in tenth-inch segments. The flammability results for any fabric must then be evaluated by local authorities—often the head of the local fire department.

Consideration must also be given to the fabric backing or substrate, which can either reduce flame spread or be very combustible itself. Flame resistance depends on both fiber content and construction. Tightly woven, smooth-surfaced fabrics tend to resist flame spread, whereas shaggy and loosely constructed fabrics encourage it.

All specified fabrics fall into one of the following four categories [(3) and (4) are referred to as "inherently flame-retardant"]:

1. *Flammable* or *inflammable* means easily set afire. Included among this category are fabrics woven of untreated cellulosic fibers such as cotton, linen, rayon, and acetate. (This classification is not to be confused with the Flammable Fabrics Act [U.S. Commercial Standard 191-53], which

outlawed such highly flammable fabrics as brushed rayons, nor with the subsequent amendment DOC FF1-70, covering carpet fabrics.)

2. *Flame-resistant* describes fabrics whose fiber content is difficult to ignite and burns slowly when ignited. Fibers with these characteristics include wool, mohair, silk (modified by weight and density), and such thermoplastics as nylons, polyesters, and olefins. It is important to recognize that resistance to flame implies no more than resistance to burning. The thermoplastic fibers do not burn easily, but they can be as dangerous in a fire as burning fabrics because they *melt*, raining hot, molten masses that ignite the more flammable fabrics and rugs within range. They sometimes release toxic fumes.

3. *Flameproof* or *nonflammable* means just that. These fabrics are constructed of glass, metal, or asbestos fibers.

4. *Fire-retardant though not fireproof* describes a group of man-made fibers, including sarans, modacrylics, and newer developments such as Kynol, Nomex, PVC, and Cordelan, which are officially acceptable for most situations.

Most fibers lacking inherent resistance to flame can be made safe with topical finishes, which are classified as durable or nondurable. A durable flame-retardant finish is defined as one that lasts through twenty-five washings or twenty dry cleanings. Flamefoe W/P (washable finish) and Flamefoe KH (dry-cleanable finish) are two common brands. (These terms postdate the earlier Pyroset and NBX, which are now used only in California.) Today, flame-retardant finishing treatments hardly ever weaken, stiffen, or change the color of a fabric. Tests to judge whether any or all of these problems will arise with any specific fabric can be made by submitting a sample to the finisher.

BEYOND THE PINCH PLEAT

The postwar era has been dominated by the curtain wall in architecture and the *curtained wall* in decoration—both with good reason. For the many offices and apartments that have only one outside wall, letting that wall be glass—all glass—to admit as much light as possible and to extend, if only by suggestion, the confining perimeter is usually completely defensible. For the designer trying to re-create Maxim's within an all-glass street-level space, the rationale still holds: it is far easier to close off windows than to open up new ones.

By the same token a wall-to-wall, floor-to-ceiling veil of casement is often sufficient to reduce glare, screen a dismal view, or unify poor fenestration—and so much better than traversing cloth a foot below the ceiling or cutting the hemline at knee level. Most of us have learned to position window fabric in terms of the room, not the fenestration. Some noble windows have been masked out in the process: too many grand views are forever veiled, while oppressing overviews intrude into living spaces. Close neighbors share secrets because windows are badly placed and inadequately treated. The pinch-pleated, postwar curtained wall is sometimes as senseless a cliché as the endless pairs of overdraperies that guarded most openings of prewar vintage—sometimes more so.

Contemporary design is supposed to be sensible and functional. Too often, it is not. Architectural planners have not considered the *inside* window elevation nor allowed for such practical problems as where to stack open draperies or how to screen out the sun without suffocating the air conditioner. Too often, the inhabitant is too baffled or hidebound to correct the situation sensibly and sensitively. The most frequent foul-up is Treating All The Windows The Same No Matter What. The most obvious example is the glass tower: when the sunny side and the sunless side are treated the same way, at least one of them is not effective. One variation is when one side of a building faces the bay, and the other a grimy facade sixty feet across the alley; another is treating the sun-crazed top levels with the same solution as those as the canyon bottom. Although the arguments for a unified facade are reasonable, uniformity can allow for variations in density within the same color, yarn, and construction.

The domestic version is not dissimilar. Although different windows within a room often have very different outlooks—or inlooks—they tend to be treated as twins. When their proportions vary ridiculously, as in the bedrooms that have "good" windows plus a small air hatch for cross-ventilation, they *must* be treated for what they are. Shutters toned to the wall color is often the simplest solution for the hatch.

Too many rooms have either a single fabric layer that is too heavy by day but too open at night—or layers that are so clumsy to operate that they presuppose servants. Windows in Roman apartments often have six layers, including a heavy outer shutter that keeps out heat and intruders, glass doors that swing completely open, veils, and heavy, padded hangings that are light- and soundproof. Too much? Maybe not. At stake are air, light, view, temperature, energy, and real and implied security. People are worthy of such consideration.

There are more ways of handling fabric than most of us utilize—even of draping fabric. There are places for shirred and smocked headings, for accordion pleating, for box and cartridge pleats. In the days when Dorothy Liebes wove custom draperies, she designed different pleatings for each one. Often the pleats snapped together so the made-up cloth could be shipped, stored, and cleaned straight out.

Europeans often finish off banks of sheer fabric with two or three four- to six-inch horizontal tucks above the hem. The weighting is useful, and the effect tailored and custom. We seldom see it in the United States, but one day layers of sheers that combine ingeniously to create a third magic dimension will be discovered.

We are all aware of window treatments that are alternatives to draped fabric, but many, especially roller shades, vertical blinds, and Roman shades, deserve wider use than they now have. When windows do not reach the ceiling but draperies do, a ceiling-hung blind between them may give the illusion of a higher, handsomer window. Blinds and shades that rise rather than lower are often useful to ensure privacy or block out visual chaos. Low, folding screens sometimes serve the same purpose, as well as hiding radiators and air conditioners.

The point is *to think, to consider*. There are no rules, but intelligence counts in a thoughtless world. Aesthetic considerations are precious.

2-3. The window treatment for Paul Rudolph's Art and Architecture building at Yale is imaginative and appropriate. The large-scale flat panels of hand-woven ropes are actually cargo nets, which are industrially produced and therefore not extremely expensive. The scale is appropriate to large spaces; the texture relates to the dominant striated concrete; the light-diffusing properties are both decorative and architectural; durability is top-notch. (Photo by Joseph Molitor.)

2. On Furniture

AESTHETIC CONSIDERATIONS

Certainly, the success of a specific piece of furniture depends on the relationship of the fabric to the character of the piece. The more positive or complex the furniture form, material, and detailing, the narrower the range of fabric that will work well with it. An easy, formless sofa may accept the widest variety of textures, colors, or patterns, while a well-defined chair with exposed wood and strong lines may limit the choice. Seating with a strong silhouette is, in effect, a piece of sculpture, and the upholstery should affirm and emphasize the form—not camouflage it.

Diversity

Upholstery fabric is the great modifier of furniture design. Fabric often determines the style and character, the scale and importance, and, to a large extent, the price and staying power of the upholstered piece. Even furniture manufacturers seldom realize the increased range of uses that upholstery may lend to their products. There are, for example, chairs so basic that their appropriateness to a particular use derives from the character of the covers.

A basic chair that in a chintz is appropriate for the boudoir may—in a wool tweed—be sufficiently masculine for a study. Tailored in leather or a ribbed worsted, this same classic chair becomes sufficiently chaste and deluxe for executive use. Upholstery techniques or styles may aid in the personality change. The boudoir chair may be skirted and rounded out with extra down; the library chair, weltless and buttoned; the executive model, channeled and saddle-stitched.

Or the relationship can be worked backwards, using fabric to soften and "make residential" contemporary furniture that is almost always designed for "contract" use. Custom and customized furniture frames are becoming ever more costly and harder to come by, and a diversified range of upholstery "bodies" is likewise becoming more difficult for manufacturers and dealers to maintain. The undifferentiated forms that are taking their place need particularization. In contrast, the variety of fabric coverings is increasing.

2-4. Edward Wormley's famous Edward Chair is upholstered in *Tyrol*, a pebbly worsted which is a textural counterpoint to the smoothness of the ash frame. Both have the same light, neutral value, which heightens the effect.

Tautness or Looseness

How upholstery frames are padded and cushioned, finished and welted is related to fabric selection, as is the degree of tautness of a fabric covering. Whether the fabric is to be tightly pulled over the cushioning to effect a hard, tailored surface or dimpled into an easy-going shapelessness should—for reasons of comfort and of fabric life—be taken into consideration in making a selection.

Flatness

The most universal requirement for patterned upholstery fabric is that the pattern must appear dimensionally flat and static. As a piece of furniture itself has form, it requires a more structured pattern with less movement and dimension than a window. Dimensional depth within the fabric pattern destroys the furniture's form and creates a busy camouflage. Two of the most common violations of this rule are dark, printed forms floating on white grounds and circular or lumpy motifs punctuating the fabric plane. Generally, any unbalanced diagonal or spiral movement is deadly.

Scale

The scale of a pattern is important in relation to both the furniture and to the space it occupies. Many of the large and violent floral prints that look so unhappy jammed into small rooms looked much better, no doubt, in the huge, sparsely furnished English manor houses for which they were intended.

Aside from the scale of the pattern, the scale of the cloth itself is important. A fragile chair covered in a thick, textured weave may appear to be wearing an overcoat. An overweight sofa in a thin weave may seem to have been caught in its underwear.

Intended Use

Fashion is a particularly inappropriate determinant in upholstery selection. The white sofa in a room that the family plans to lounge in and the pastel silk in the sorority drawing room are deplorable not simply because soiling and damage are likely but also because they discourage the intended use of the room. To be sure, some white upholstery schemes are less inappropriate than they might appear at first glance. The posh white upholstery of an executive lounge is an example of this kind of installation. It is calculated, no doubt, to discourage all but the highest echelons to actually use the space—it exists only to impress visitors. In planning a house for a young couple in San Francisco, Frances Mihailoff upholstered rare Venetian antiques with white Naugahyde. Decorative interest was in the ornate frames and in wall objects placed well above the reach of small hands. The silk covers were reinstated after the children were grown.

Sense of Touch

Because upholstery fabrics are not merely looked at but also touched and sat upon, how they feel is almost as important as their appearance.

Perhaps it is because modern man has lost his lively awareness of touch that most upholstery fabrics today are fairly neutral in hand. They are neither too rough nor overly slippery, neither pleasant nor unpleasant; they stimulate neither sensuous pleasure nor revulsion. We tend to forget that certain combinations of yarn and construction produce fabrics of marked sensuous appeal. Obvious examples are heavy satins and silk velvets. Less obvious but just as pleasant are the stimulating textures of spongy, ribbed, and corded weaves.

Comfort

In rooms where people spend many hours at a time, the unrelenting monotony of certain plastic-coated fabrics should be thought about realistically before a choice is made. Similarly, prickly, harsh fabrics are especially irritating in hot, humid climates. Even where air conditioning keeps atmospheric conditions under control, their textures may create tense hostilities.

Porosity

The ease with which air and moisture can pass through a cloth is important—in direct proportion to the length of time the occupant is in contact with the upholstery. For a café dining chair the ability of a fabric to "breathe" may not be so important; for a lounge or office chair, it is crucial.

A fabric's ability to breathe is a relative rather than an absolute characteristic—few materials are totally nonporous. From cane to loose, open weaves, through which air passes readily, to tight-set weaves, leathers, or backed films, there is an enormous range of porosity. Porosity is sometimes adversely affected by protective finishes—any finish should be checked before treatment. The ability to breathe is affected by the density of fabric construction and the material of the cushioning beneath the upholstery. Thus, cotton batting over springs will obviously interfere less with air passage than a thick, dense foam. If the fabric is not porous, sinking into a deep sofa will produce dampness and discomfort faster than perching on a side chair covered in the same fabric.

PHYSICAL PROPERTIES

Life Expectancy

It is important not to lose sight of the fact that the durability of an upholstery fabric is the sum total of not one but many physical qualities. Although resistance to abrasion is perhaps the most essential durability factor, selecting upholstery for this quality alone may entail the risk of having a faded, uncleanable, or nonbreathing fabric that lasts *too* long. The real staying power of fabric must be measured not in terms of hole-free, grimy dead-beats but of a sense of life and a responsiveness to cleaning. Indeed, some fabrics—leathers and silk velvets come to mind—age gracefully. In these cloths the patina of use is more characterful than shabby.

2-5. These Irish upholsteries, shown full-scale, combine yarn and weave interest. In this fancy herringbone, slubby Irish-wool filling contrasts with a black warp. There is a pleasant consistency in the yarn and the random-weave pattern.

2-6. *Academia* employs the same characterful wool yarn in a double cloth. The ground cloth has a wool warp and weft; the recessed insets are of a fine metallic gimp yarn.

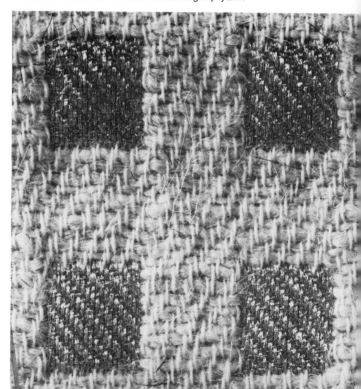

Snagging

Snagging is catching and pulling a yarn out of the cloth surface. If a loop is formed or a single yarn breaks, it is generally not a serious problem. Knitted and loop-pile fabrics, especially, should be remedied immediately so that a longer pull or run does not occur. Depending on the scale and the type of construction, mending may consist of pushing the loop to the reverse side of the cloth, darning broken ends into the mesh of the cloth, or neatly clipping them off. Occasional snagging is not serious, but if it is frequent or covers broad areas of the cloth, it is menacing indeed. Even though backings, especially heavy latex, tend to reduce snagging, upholsteries with long floats or with open loops of slippery yarns are at best "residential." Pets are chief offenders, and people are especially prone to pick at fabric when they are idle or nervous.

Abrasion Resistance

Resistance to abrasion is directly related to the form and the construction of the furniture, to the yarn and the construction of the fabric itself, and to the amount and the type of use. Use is not taken into consideration as often as it should be. A realistic appraisal must involve function: seating in waiting rooms or lobbies will be used heedlessly as well as constantly.

One must anticipate the practical necessity of replacing upholstery when abrasion begins to destroy the fabric at some vulnerable point on a chair or sofa. Invariably, this point is the arm. Upholstery can be expected to last twice as long on a chair or sofa without arms or with exposed wooden ones. Depending on chair height and pitch, the next weak point is the top, front edge of the seat, particularly if there is a welt. Welts themselves are points of wear because they are raised above the overall surface and because the fabric covering the welt is stretched and uncushioned.

Abrasion is a grinding action, largely affected by the resilience of the undercushioning. A soft cushioning takes the brunt of the impact, protecting the covering fabric. Another factor is the de-

gree to which the fabric is stretched. The more tightly it is pulled, the more vulnerable it becomes.

A specific fabric's resistance to abrasion is affected by the type and quality of the fiber; the size, twist, and ply of the yarn; the density of the weave; and, to some extent, the finish and backing. Hard, impervious yarns such as horsehair and synthetic monofilaments provide a strong surface, as do tightly twisted and plied yarns, because each ply within the yarn strand is protected by the overlapping of the following ply. Similarly, a close-set weave will provide a resistant surface. Here, the individual yarns are protected by the unified surface of a cohesive weave. The weight or thickness of the fabric is also a factor. The built-in, cushioning resilience of a thick, soft fabric tends to give it durability.

Tests for abrasion resistance are frequently used by fiber and fabric manufacturers. For extensive installations tests are often performed at the request of specifiers. Although they are inconclusive and abstract, the two best-known methods are the Taber and Wyzenbeek tests (see Part 5, section 1).

Fuzzing and Pilling

Abrasion causes several other kinds of fabric failure. *Fuzzing*, the result of fibers working out of the fabric onto the surface, creates an unsightly, soil-collecting condition. When these fibers roll into balls, the condition is called *pilling*. Pilling is common to certain wool fabrics, but because it can be expected to diminish, it is not considered a difficulty. The problem is more crucial with synthetic fibers such as spun nylon, which are so strong and tenacious that the pills refuse to fall off. Moreover, they always become dirty. Fuzzing and pilling will seriously mar the surface of these fabrics, so they should be avoided. If a tendency to fuzz or pill is discovered too late—after the furniture has been upholstered—hand shearing is the only expedient.

Color Abrasion

Loss of color due to abrasion occurs if there has been poor dye penetration. Hard, dye-resisting linen fibers have been a principal cause for complaint. But color abrasion occurs with cottons and some synthetics as well, and in both woven and printed fabrics. It is only slightly more common in piece-dyed goods than in yarn-dyed ones. It is more noticeable with dark colors than with light shades that approximate the natural yarn color. It is more problematic in prints with allover coverage than in those interrupted by areas of natural ground color. A nubby surface that exposes portions of the fabric ground with intensified wear is particularly vulnerable to color abrasion.

Upholsteries with welts, very tightly stretched fabric, or hard cushioning, which are vulnerable to abrasion, are also subject to color abrasion. In other words, color abrasion is caused by the same conditions as any other abrasion. To avoid it, check out not only the fabric but furniture wear points such as arm edges, etc., and watch out for susceptible constructions.

Occasionally, printed or piece-dyed upholstery fabric exhibits a fault resembling color abrasion. Tiny flecks of the undyed surface are revealed when movement causes a slight shift of the woven yarns.

Crocking

Crocking, not a common fault, is excess dyestuff rubbing off a fabric onto to some other surface, such as, alas! a new white suit. But despite initial fears, only the excess dye rubs off, and you will rarely end up with a colorless fabric.

Actually, there are two kinds of crocking—dry and wet. Either is usually temporary. Dry crocking may occur with fabrics such as wool tweeds as residual oils containing dyestuff rub off. Certain leathers and many suedes crock—a familiar complaint with ladies' handbags and gloves. The condition usually does not last long. Wet crocking is another matter. Triggered by perspiration or rain-wet clothes, excess dye will rub off onto other materials.

If the frame of a new piece of furniture is pushed against a freshly painted wall during installation, a streak of color may result, but this does not mean that the fabric will crock. A simple test for crocking is to rub the questionable fabric with a clean, white cotton cloth—a handkerchief will do.

Tensile Strength

Fibers, yarns, and fabrics vary in tensile strength. Low tensile strength, which results in tears and splitting, is not a common hazard of upholstery fabric. Flameproofing or other finishes may cause deterioration, making the fabric so *tender* that it will split or tear. Sun rot is another evil. Occasionally velvets and plushes become tender in dyeing or finishing.

Dimensional Stability

Dimensional stability, or shape retention, is more important in an upholstery fabric than in a drapery because correcting the failure is more complex and costly. Upholstery fabric is expected to fit furniture without buckling, sagging, or wrinkling. These failures occur when the upholstery fabric stretches or simply lacks resilience—the ability to expand and shrink back to its normal contour after the occupant leaves. In this case resilience and dimensional stability may be considered to be the same.

What is often diagnosed as fabric sagging and stretching is actually the shrinkage or deformation of the undercushion. New foams and experimental furniture shapes have increased the likelihood of this failure. In sculptured furniture and unbuttoned slab cushioning, where the outline must be maintained without reinforcement, fabric resilience is vital. Fabrics lacking either resilience or stability should be supported by buttoning, channeling, or tufting.

Resistance to Slippage

Warp or filling yarns will occasionally slide or slip over each other. Although slippage is infrequent in upholstery cloths, it is a serious fault. It not only makes the surface look untidy, but more important, the fabric will become vulnerable to rapid destruction from abrasion. Chief offenders are slippery yarns such as silk and man-made filaments and loose or imbalanced fabric constructions. The best insurance against slippage is to sufficiently back fabrics that are prone to the problem (see below).

The most troublesome form of slippage is seam slippage. Here, the seaming stitches hold firm, but the adjacent yarns pull away. Because seam slippage can rarely be corrected, it must be prevented with a backing. Almost as troublesome are yarns raveling out at the cut edge. Both problems may happen in the same fabric. With heavy, hand-woven fabrics, some finer silk ones, or fabrics of synthetic filaments, raveling may be so severe that the entire seam allowance will shred.

Workroom procedures to overcome both seam slippage and raveling include the following: (1) allow ample width for seams—at least one-half to three-quarters of an inch; (2) machine-stitch the outline of the pattern before cutting; (3) seam with a double row of tight machine stitches; and (4) reinforce seams by stitching muslin to the seam areas.

BACKINGS

The business of *backing* (back-coating) fabrics has become a sizable, sophisticated, and specialized industry. There are several reasons for this. An increasing number of inexpensive fabrics are so poorly constructed that only a heavy back coating will hold them together. Further, a number of luxury fabrics such as silks and unfinished wool weaves gain in hand and stability with an appropriate backing. In either case the backing tends to make the fabric easier to cut and sew. In some cases it is only the backing that renders the fabric sufficiently stable or resistant to slippage and raveling.

STRETCH FABRICS

Stretch fabrics for upholstery were unheard-of before the sixties. They may revolutionize not only upholstery techniques but furniture design itself. New furniture shapes—free-flowing, organic, anatomically determined—may now be built by both traditional methods of joining, webbing, padding, and tacking and less conventional methods such as covering the frame with a foam pad and tightly pulling a stretch fabric over everything or casting a monolithic seating unit and pulling a skin-tight fabric over it. This girdlelike approach to upholstery is infinitely easier, quicker, and less costly. Even on conventional furniture stretch fabrics permit better fit with fewer and less meticulous seams.

The greatest advantage of stretch-fabric upholstery is the ease with which removable covers can be engineered. This opens up the possibility of changing covers at will—and removing them, like sweaters, for full-immersion cleaning. In places where removal of chairs is particularly inconvenient or even impossible, as in auditoriums and mass-transit facilities, the advantage is inestimable. Snug-fitting slipcovers can be changed or replaced without shop time for a custom upholsterer or transport charges. The potential of stretch fabrics has hardly been explored. Their heyday will come when furniture shapes are cast, and the covers will be one-piece, full-fashion knits as easy to pull on and off as stockings or gloves.

Range

The range of stretch fabrics available on the market nowadays is already larger than most designers realize—and the choice is growing rapidly. There are tricot and double knits; and flat, textured, patterned, and pile-woven stretch fabrics. Both knits and weaves can be printed, although the possibility of distortion limits pattern selection somewhat. Most of these constructions are made with true two-way stretch or a modification in which the stretch element is in only one direction.

Although two-way stretch is sometimes desirable for contouring the compound curves of sculptured upholstery, a modified two-way stretch with fifteen percent elongation is usually adequate. The key is not stretch (elongation) but *return*, or the stamina to pull back and keep smoothly taut. In addition, stretch fabrics must meet all the physical and aesthetic requirements of their intended use. (The characteristics of stretch yarns are described in Part 3, section 3.)

Dependability

We have long since passed the point where technological innovation outweighs the disadvantage of possible failure. One can be too timid and refuse to use stretch upholsteries on the ground that they might sag before the furniture wears out. The authors have never known this to happen with a carefully sewn stretch fabric.

As many stretch fabrics have come out of apparel technology, the scale of pattern or texture is often that of garments—overly flat, overly smooth, unarchitectural. As the demand for stretch fabrics stimulates the production of a larger design and texture repertory, we are seeing many sleazy fabrics that are unsuitable in yarn and density. They will stretch and perhaps return but will not resist soil and abrasion.

Application

At the time of this writing many furniture manufacturers are not enthusiastic about receiving stretch fabric as com (customers' own material). They are accustomed to cutting fabric to patterns designed for nonstretch fabrics and do not know how to calculate the stretch allowance. The custom upholsterer may also balk, but he can more readily adjust his cutting standards. It is not necessary for the workroom to handle all stretch fabrics as a special problem. Many can be handled like conventional fabrics.

When you are specifying stretch fabric to be used for upholstery, it may be necessary to submit a trial sample in advance for approval. If the factory upholsterer has used it before, he may arrive at some guidelines for the yardage requirements—otherwise, he may need to make a full-size mock-up.

UPHOLSTERY MAINTENANCE

Maintenance should be considered in regard to both the fabric selected and what is reasonable for the maintenance staff at hand. Regular vacuuming and prompt removal of spots is so essential to good upholstery maintenance that some design offices are writing a spot-and-stain-removal kit into their specifications. Some old and deep-seated stains can be removed—but with great difficulty.

Science has provided us with a wide array of beautiful and useful fabrics. But sophisticated finishes and man-made fibers compound maintenance problems.

For example, rayon and olefins have an opposite rate of absorbency. Highly absorbent rayon responds to cleaning fluids, but it absorbs many types of moisture-borne soil; hydrophobic olefins repel both cleaning fluids and certain types of moisture-laden soil. Some fabrics shrink; the dyes of others can bleed or fade. Water-soluble sizings, used for visual effect, can dissolve, leaving permanent surface marks or blotches. Some cleaning fluids can release the chemicals or dyes concealed in underlinings or backings—foams in particular. Too much moisture can bring the crayon markings used as cutting guides to the surface. These will continue to appear, with an "x-ray" effect.

Those cherished repellent finishes, Scotchgard and Zepel, need special care. With time and hard wear minuscule cracks, scratches, or roughened surfaces can develop. Dirt becomes embedded within these separations, creating a particularly severe and chronic cleaning problem.

Velvet presents an atypical problem—it should never be spot-cleaned. Instead, it responds well to damp fluffing and brushing—an exclusively professional technique.

All spills should be blotted immediately with a clean cloth. Catching liquid before it seeps into the fabric saves grief later. If old spots and stains must be cleaned or spotted on the premises, the cleaning agent should first be carefully tested on a small, inconspicuous place on the back or bottom of the chair or sofa, and the following suggestions should be taken into consideration: (1) for oil-borne stains use a petroleum-based dry-cleaning solvent (such as the Stoddart System), which is a derivative of gasoline and kerosene, perchloroethylene, or K_2R, a chlorine derivative; (2) for water-borne stains spot-clean very carefully with small amounts of water; (3) for fabrics with a hard surface try an art-gum eraser; (4) for stains on cotton slipcovers launder *only* if the fabric is preshrunk and colorfast. (Caution: do not use a petroleum-based solvent on fabrics upholstered over foam rubber.)

SPECIFICATION OF UPHOLSTERY FABRICS

Except for furniture bought as shown, at least some of these points apply whenever fabric is purchased. Even when fabric is selected on a furniture floor, there are frequent misunderstandings, which on delivery lead to, "But I thought the stripes would run vertically!"

Direction

Fabrics as they come off the bolt have four directions and two sides, the *face* and the *back*. Completely nondirectional fabrics such as felt and some plain weaves can be upholstered either horizontally or vertically, even on the same piece of furniture. At the other extreme some patterned fabrics such as those with stemmed flowers permit only one top, which is usually obvious enough to prevent error. If the top is at all subtle, specific directions must be given.

Directional fabrics such as stripes and striae can most often be run in either direction. Satin stripes, an exception, should be vertical. A vertical stripe run standardly will remain vertical. If it is *railroaded*, or run on its side, the stripes will be horizontal. Instructions should state whether the stripes are to run vertically or horizontally.

Cut-pile fabrics, such as velvet and velour, and napped fabrics, such as suedecloth, are standardly run with the pile direction slanting down on vertical planes and toward the front on horizontal planes. Fabrics with a float direction, such as satins, or with a ridge direction, such as horsehair or corduroy, provide more comfort and wear better when the ridge runs vertically.

Stripes, particularly horizontal stripes, often fail to match. If they can be run vertically or specified so that match is not essential, considerable grief and wasted effort will be avoided.

Pattern Placement

The placement of the pattern should be considered and specified. Some patterns are designed to appear repeatless. As it is standard upholstery practice to spot the same motif for each pillow and chair back, it is necessary to instruct the upholsterer to let random designs fall where they will. If sofa pillows *are* to match pattern, this needs to be specified, and extra fabric allowed for it.

Face

Most decorative fabrics are finished to one side, the face. Even weaves that are two-sided in structure are mended to the face side and more and more frequently coated on the reverse side. Trade practice is to roll the fabric with the face on the *inside* of the bolt. Most fabric houses also label the face. Instructions to the upholsterer should specify *face side out*.

Writing the Specification

The fabric should be completely identified by both name and number. This will help prevent possible errors. If both yardage and price have been specified and extended, the specifier will be notified about unexpected changes in price. Shipping directions should be clear, with thorough and exact information in the *mark for* blank.

The specifier is not necessarily the purchaser: more and more frequently they are *not* the same. The specifier's name and firm should be on the purchase order to enable the fabric house to get the specifier's approval of match and other requirements. Of course, specifications should include instructions regarding welts—whether they should be used and if so, what kind; buttoning; extra arm pads, if desired; and where to send the remainder of the goods, if any.

3. On Walls and Ceilings

Whereas fabric is the universal covering for windows and furniture, until recently it was unusual to find it on walls and ceilings. That fabric appears more frequently on walls today is the result of physical or psychic need. While it has long been agreed that contemporary rooms need texture, pattern, and color, a return to focusing on the surrounding itself (rather than on objects within) is quite recent.

Part of the intent is to reinforce, compensate, or supplant architectural detailing or structural materials, which today are at best minimal. Dry-wall construction and factory-made wall panels have only aggravated the monotony of bare walls. And whether space is designed for work, living, or pleasure, the need to make it personal is as important as relieving the monotony.

When the furnishings within bland spaces such as offices and hospitals are mass-produced with "easy-care" surfaces, the walls can offer tactile and psychic relief. Embossed-vinyl wall coverings, although they *may* be cleanable, are unfulfilling, and although wallpapers range from pretty to jazzy, they too offer neither the textural nor the tactile variety available with fabric. Nor do they offer any variety in installation techniques.

The range of fabric textures available offers a broad choice of easily applied aesthetic effects for the interior designer to exploit. Perhaps more significant than the surface texture of any specific fabric is the malleability, suppleness, and warmth of fabric as an alternative material to such surfacings as wood, tile, brick, marble, or paper. Fabric brings a nestlike softness to the interior it encloses that is physically and psychologically satisfying. The sensuous, tactile pleasure of feeling the fabric's surface is enhanced by the gentle "give" of a yielding, plumply padded wall, which feels so different from the forbidding hardness of other wall surfaces.

A most effective and economical use of fabric is to cover up badly finished, cracked, or uneven walls when time, funds, or labor for a complete plastering are lacking.

As a ceiling treatment fabric modifies the proportions of a space. It is most often used to lower a ceiling that is too high. Dramatic examples are the tent canopies that were hung in Malmaison during the Napoleonic Empire. The fabric focused attention on the impressiveness of the room's lofty proportions. Because today's standard ceilings are so low, fabrics are rarely hung in major rooms.

In making a selection, remember that even the costliest fabrics are far less expensive to install—and to remove—than stone, marble, or choice woods. Although perimeter walls may seem long, the wall fabric will be stretched out its full measure, not gathered to one-half or one-third its width as in draperies.

2-7. This hand-woven wall fabric combines a ribbon of fused yarns with a weft of raffia alternated with copper wire. The total construction suggests flatness, reflects light back into the room, and is easy to maintain. Designed by Marjatta Metsovaara.

2-8. *Muralto*, a wall fabric, is a gargantuan waffle weave of heavy natural-colored wool yarns. It is so thick and dense that it creates air pockets that drink up noise and modulate sound. The structural relief of highlight and shadow dispels the monotony of smooth walls or conceals old walls that are cracked or pitted. The 102-inch width is designed to be applied horizontally without seams, so it can be removed for immersion cleaning or moved to another location.

FUNCTIONS OF WALL AND CEILING FABRICS

Acoustical Control

Fabric is useful both in reducing the volume of sound reverberations within a room and in preventing the transmission of sound from one room or area to another. If the cloth itself does not deaden sound sufficiently, it may be augmented by sound-absorbing batting or acoustical board behind the decorative fabric. In some instances fabric laminated to foam is sufficiently porous to tone down sound waves.

The psychological effect of quiet—the impression of intimacy, remoteness, and serenity that one finds in thickly upholstered rooms—reinforces the tangible, measurable sound control achieved by a fabric treatment. Upholstered rooms not only reduce the decibel count of conversation but make the average occupant lower his voice unconsciously. The reduction of incidental and reflected sound makes lower voices audible.

Concealing Nail Holes

Unpatterned, textured wall fabrics are a frequent choice in galleries and collectors' homes. They not only provide richness and interest on what must of necessity be a plain surface, but they also conceal nail holes and ubiquitous haloes that result from removing or changing pictures and other wall-hung art objects.

Richly patterned fabrics are often at their best laid flat. Drapery folds or cutting may detract from their beauty. Stretched flat over large areas or used to line bays and alcoves, such fabrics are honestly exploited as applied ornament of the most straightforward kind.

2-9. This wall fabric is a warp laminate of wool yarns adhered to a paper backing. Its effect is softly naturalistic and tactile. It is sound-absorbing and resistant to soil and bruises.

METHODS OF INSTALLATION

Technology has made great advances in applying fabric to walls and ceilings since the Napoleonic Empire. Alternative methods of installation allow aesthetic as well as practical maneuverability.

Paste-up Techniques

A direct *paste-up* technique is used with (a) paper-backed, (b) foam-backed, and (c) acrylic back-coated fabric. Paste-up techniques are the simplest and among the least expensive. The limitations are: (1) unsophisticated paperhangers may not be up to the job; (2) to laminate without bias or bow is difficult, especially with soft fabric; (3) fabrics with a horizontal match such as stripes or plaids are not recommended (in this respect paper-backing, which allows for no adjustment in hanging, is too problematic to consider); and (4) because the trimmed edge is exposed, weaves with heavy yarns may tend to ravel.

(a) In paper-backing a heavy, easy-to-*strip* (remove from the wall) paper is laminated to the fabric, which is then hung like wallpaper with a water-based adhesive. Warp-laminated fabrics such as the one shown in figure 2-9 are applied in this way. As there is no horizontal match and the vertical warps conceal the seam, the paste-up method is ideal.

(b) In the foam-laminate process one-eighth- to one-quarter-inch flame-retardant foam is laminated to the fabric. The foam adds stability without totally sacrificing "give," which may be useful in installation. On the wall the foam pad adds a soft resilience and additional sound absorption. The foam-laminated fabric is hung with a vinyl adhesive.

(c) An acrylic back coating is applied to the fabric both to stabilize it and to prevent the adhesive from wicking through to the surface. Many upholstery cloths come with a suitable acrylic backing. If not, one can be applied as a special finish (see Part 3, section 5). To hang the fabric, a vinyl adhesive is applied to the wall—not to the fabric. Plastic-coating a fabric, which is sometimes done to match bathroom walls to a bedroom or a pantry to the dining area, also enables it to hang as a wall fabric.

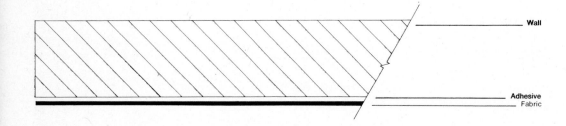

Wall

Adhesive
Fabric

2-10.

Upholstered Fabric Walls

This method of application is the most traditional and foolproof of all. It is also the easiest to move or take down for cleaning. Simple wood laths are nailed to the wall at the perimeter of the area to be covered. The fabric widths are seamed side by side prior to mounting. The whole fabric panel is then stretched tightly as it is stapled to the laths. To cover the staples, a decorative molding, braid, or welt may be applied. A double welt, which can be invisibly stapled through its center, is simple and effective.

If the wall itself is sufficiently soft (and expendable) to support the staples, even the lath can be eliminated. In most instances with most fabrics, however, a thin batting or cloth lining under the fabric will create a softer hand and a more sumptuous look. This lining is either pasted to the wall or seamed and stapled.

Panels with Blind-tacked Seams

This technique is similar to the one just described but dispenses with sewing. It is particularly suitable for thin fabrics. The effect is crisp and tailored. To hold the staples or protect the wall, vertical laths may be attached to the wall at intervals corresponding to the width of the finished panels.

As shown in figure 2-12, first staple the wrong side of the leftmost panel. Over this staple line staple a one-inch strip of stiff cardboard. This will produce a knife-edge fold in the fabric as it is pulled over the cardboard and stretched to the next lath in line. This process is repeated across the entire wall. The right edge of the right-hand panel must be blind-tacked or covered with molding. The top and bottom raw edges can be stapled and covered by a molding or blind-nailed into place.

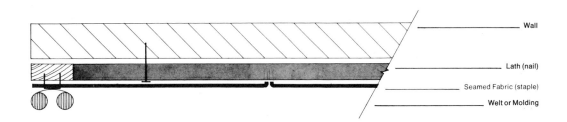

2-11.

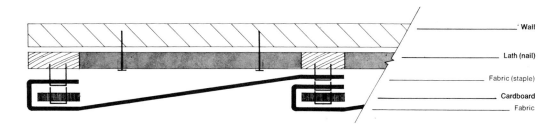

2-12.

Solid-wrapped Panels

Of all techniques, this one is the most architectural. It has the added advantage that the fabric is removable for dry cleaning or replacement. A three-quarter-inch panel of wood, chipboard, or Homosote is wrapped with fabric that is tightly stapled to the panel's wrong side. Unless the fabric itself is thick and spongy, a batting or fabric padding should be wrapped and stapled over the panel underneath the fabric. As shown in figure 2-13, a tapered offset molding may be added to true the edge and give depth to the panel reveal. The finished panel is then attached to the wall with mechanical fasteners. These panels are often *floated* on the wall, i.e., mounted with a space of up to half an inch between each other and between them and the ceiling. Often up to two inches are left at the floor line. The infinitesimal amount of wall left showing is painted shadow gray.

The J. B. Associates System

This proprietary system involves mounting fabric on an invisible frame, which in turn is attached to a wall-mounted lath frame by means of patented hidden fasteners. Any fabric, with or without backing, can be used. A thick, sound-absorbing padding can be used within the frame. (Approved by the fire codes of New York, Boston, and California, the J. B. Associates System is available through Homecraft Drapery and Upholstery Corporation in New York City and its licensed representatives.)

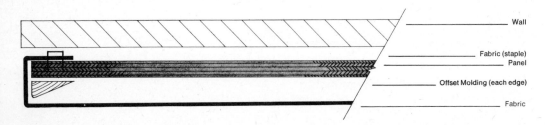

Wall
Fabric (staple)
Panel
Offset Molding (each edge)
Fabric

2-13.

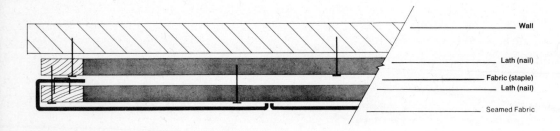

Wall
Lath (nail)
Fabric (staple)
Lath (nail)
Seamed Fabric

2-14.

Guidelines

When you are having wall fabrics backed with either paper or foam, confidence in the laminator is essential. Errors in alignment cannot be corrected by the paperhanger. As it is unlikely that lamination will be accurately on-grain with the fabric, prints and embroideries are not recommended for this process. On the other hand, if the fabric has been given only a light acrylic backing—enough to prevent the glue from penetrating to the surface but not enough to lock the fibers into alignment—small adjustments can be made in stretching or compacting the fabric during the hanging process. In either case, once the fabric is hung by the paper-, acrylic-, or foam-backed technique, it cannot be changed or adjusted.

A few words of caution are in order if wall fabric is installed by one of the panel-hung or upholstered-panel techniques. Patterned and striped fabrics offer the special challenge of matching. Alertness to the problem and constant checking is recommended.

As horizontal yarns have a tendency to sag or pucker, the fabric must be pulled taut, and care must be taken to keep the fabric plumb and on-grain. As even preshrunk cotton will absorb sufficient atmospheric moisture to bag after hanging, it is wise to upholster or panel-wrap fabrics in atmospheric conditions similar to those on the installation location—or, more to the point, in the maximum humidity that the room will be subjected to.

Most fabric walls are amazingly resistant to both soiling and bruising. In some cases fire-retarding treatments are required. Many fabrics, especially cellulosics, that have been treated for flame retardance are so hydrophilic that they will stretch in humid conditions. Misting such fabrics so that they are stretched while damp is a wise precaution.

As the success of the fabric-covered wall rests in the hands of the coater, the laminator, or the hanger, it is wise to protect yourself with a firm written agreement—despite his commitment and integrity. Always ask for a guarantee that the fabric will be replaced if the work is not up to written specifications. On the other hand, if the laminator does not feel that the fabric will meet the specifications, he has the right to refuse the job and return the fabric.

PART 3: FABRIC FACTS

3-1. Three furnishing tweeds (bawneens) of Irish wool combine easily and naturally. The counterpane at top derives from a damasklike reversal of warp-face and filling-face cloths. The center has the same construction but is all filling face. The fret pattern below, in the same yarn but plied double, is a fancy twill with a long repeat for maximum variation.

1. Cloths

The term *cloth* includes all pliable planes, regardless of the type of fiber or the mode of construction. Cloths may be knitted or knotted, woven or non-woven, inexpensive or costly. In general, the term does not include nonfibrous films, such as vinyl sheeting, or stiff mattings, heavy blankets, or carpets.

Chintz, tweed, calico, voile, satin—there are perhaps a hundred cloths in common enough usage to be familiar to the average person. But because cloth names are "first names," the ability to connect a cloth with a name is of little help in relating one cloth to another. As it is, we speak of cloths in terms of fiber (wool, nylon, silk), weave (damask, jacquard, velvet), or finish (glazed chintz). Although this "first-name" jargon is used throughout industry and trade, it is only useful to those who know the family connections. These connections and relationships are described on the following pages.

Once this framework is understood, additional knowledge will increase understanding rather than confusion. Remember, however, that it does not indicate the sensual attributes that are the essence of all decorative fabrics. The sensible approach to selecting cloth should be, "I love it!" Will it meet the practical requirements? How can I budget in order to afford it?"

The most encompassing term is *fabric*. It embraces the whole gamut of cloths, plus rugs and carpets, tapestries, mattings, caning, wire fencing, and compound structures such as quilts and laminates. Paper, a felt of cellulosic fiber, is a fabric in this sense. Leather is a natural fabric constructed of protein fibers. To think in such broad terms helps to comprehend fabrics as a whole. It is even more useful in understanding the synthesis of new ones.

Textiles, a specific term, refer to woven fabrics. Weaving is defined as the interlacing of two or more elements in a right-angle relationship. Thirty years ago, almost all fabrics were textiles woven on a loom of some type (see Part 3, section 4). Since then, the industry's need for faster production has resulted in a broader use of nonwoven fabrics such as knits, films, felts, and the more complex laminates and tufted carpets.

Fabric, the first craft to be industrialized, is now in a second industrial phase. Simply stated, the trend is toward producing a finished consumer product from fiber with as few in-between steps as possible. A felt hat is the ultimate example: all the yarn-making steps are eliminated, and construction is at its most basic. Cutting and sewing and their incumbent waste have been replaced by a molded fabric, which is the finished product. The rubber glove goes a step further—the fiber phase is eliminated. The same is true of lounge seating formed of self-skinning plastic foams. Fully fashioned knits such as hosiery made of continuous filament yarns are thoroughly modern fabrics, particularly when the thermoplastic properties of the yarn are employed for shaping and sizing. Nonwoven fabrics are modern in terms of economy of production. They will become more so and more prevalent as better means are found to mold and bond them without sewing.

It is comforting to many people that such interesting new developments will reach the decorative-fabric field *last*. The notion of synthetic, nonwoven fabrics is to many about as savory as artificial insemination. But nonwovens need not be ugly—hornets' nests, silk cocoons, and spiders' webs are not. Actually, the specifier and the consumer will have some voice in shaping these new developments: computerization makes each purchase a ballot, and the public will get more of whatever it accepts, less of what it rejects.

For the public the new fabric technology seems to have two very diverse aspects: (1) the limitations of new technology, especially in its early phases, foster great appreciation for yarns and constructions that have functioned so well and so long as to be taken for granted; and (2) real mass production may help to make some luxury fabrics affordable to a wider audience. Just as a young professional may, by not spending her budget on nylon stockings, be able to afford handmade shoes, cashmeres, or silks, so the savings from common-denominator furnishings can subsidize some extraordinary fabrics.

The key to understanding cloth is to know the elements of its construction. An *element* is not necessarily a single yarn end: it may be a set of yarns that behave in like manner. For instance, in a simple knit there is only one element, the yarn that loops horizontally across the goods. A plain weave has two elements: one set of parallel warp yarns running vertically along the length of the cloth and another set of weft or filling yarns interlacing horizontally, or at right angles, to the warp (see Part 3, section 4).

Terrycloth and most pile weaves have a third, supplementary element, which forms a pile. Double cloths have two sets of warps and two sets of wefts, which add up to four elements. A wilton carpet has a basic warp (one element), a basic weft (one element), and, to control the pattern in the pile, up to five sets of supplementary warps. At the other extreme, as we have seen, there are fabrics with no elements: felts, and, in a broad sense, papers and leathers, nonwoven fabrics and films. Chart 2 categorizes the major fabric constructions in terms of their elemental structure.

2. Fibers

RELATIVITY

As the basic component of cloth, fiber is important—but not *all*-important. It is certainly not important in the arbitrary sense of selecting a fabric because it is cotton, wool, or nylon. What is important is *which* cotton, wool, or nylon? How *much* of it? How is it spun, constructed, finished? And for what end use?

The most common error we make is to search for mythical fiber absolutes—the fiber that does everything *well*. There is none, although fiber manufacturers suggest it repeatedly and expensively. No single fiber type, even if it is abstracted from questions of quality, construction, and end use, is endowed with universal strength. All fabrics made of any fiber will fade and soil. Some of the toughest in terms of tensile strength and abrasion resistance will quickly disintegrate in sunlight, and others that resist both sun and fire are weaklings when faced with abrasion.

Fiber producers are not the only sustaining voice for fiber absolutism. Famous decorators speak of cotton as *the* fiber; most architects swear by wool. This is misleading. What they are telling us is that certain specific cottons or wools meet the stringent demands of their own eye, hand, and experience.

We are well past the nineteen-fifties, when it was believed that some new fiber would be developed—or already had been—that would possess eternal youth. Experience has shown us that the older fibers, whether natural or man-made, are better buys—because we know them.

QUALITY

Natural fibers are the product of thousands of years of selection and crossbreeding. In all cases they have been around long enough for their attributes and limitations to be generally known. There are no myths to be dispelled but instead a certain innocence about fiber quality. For decades conventional wisdom has decreed an aristocratic hierarchy of fibers in which silk was prestigious, and cotton common. Even in the abstract this is most erroneous. The cottonlike noil silk described below, for instance, is relatively inexpensive, while such silky, extra-long-staple cottons as pima are expensive. The "pure-virgin-wool" label has excluded some of the lower grades of wool. Still, some virgin-wool fibers are three times as valuable as others. The indignation in, "Why is this twelve-ounce cloth so much more expensive than that one?" may be a show of ignorance.

Fiber snobbery carries over into man-mades and

is just as often unfair to the fiber itself. Man-made fibers are usually spun, constructed, finished, and styled for the mass market. To save steps and pennies, quality is sidestepped, and the fiber short-changed.

FIBER TERMS

A few fiber terms are so universal and so basic that they should be common knowledge.

Generic fibers refer to classifiable, chemically distinct families or "races" of fiber, such as nylon. The generic classifications are universal (see Chart 1). In contrast to trade-name fibers such as Antron (one of Du Pont's brand-name nylons), generic classifications are always written in lowercase.

Man-made is a useful term that encompasses synthetic fibers such as nylon and polyester, regenerated-cellulose fibers such as rayon, and a mineral fiber, glass.

A *filament* is a continuous fiber. In nature the only textile filaments are reeled silk and horsehair. All man-made fibers start out as filaments, which are produced from a solution extruded through a minute nozzle called a *spinneret*.

Staple fibers, like cotton and wool, vary in length according to species or breed. Man-made staple is produced from continuous filaments that are cut into specified short lengths. To become yarns, all staple fibers must be processed and spun (see Part 3, section 3).

Thermoplastic fibers soften with the application of heat. To a limited degree the natural-protein fibers—silk and wool—have this property. Acetate, a man-made cellulosic fiber, and all synthetic fibers are thermoplastic and will melt or fuse at sufficiently high temperatures. If temperature tolerances are disregarded or exeeded in treatment or pressing, fabrics will be damaged. At a lower temperature, however, fabrics can be *heat-set* to stabilize dimensions against shrinking or stretching or to emboss surface designs or configurations on a flat surface. Thermoplastic properties make permanent press and permanent pleats possible, since the heat treatment endows the fabric with "memory"—the ability to return to its heat-set form after washing or any other disruptive manipulation.

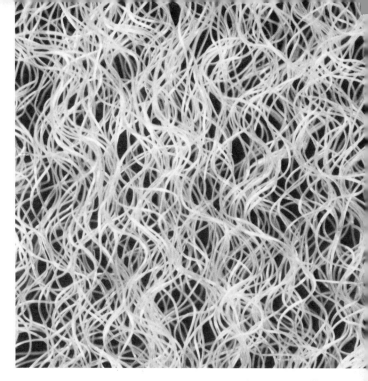

3-2. This enlarged photograph of a texturized filament yarn illustrates how the individual fibers have been curled to increase resilience and bulk. (Photo courtesy Monsanto Chemical Company.)

3-3. Two monofilament yarns are used in this warp-knit casement. The horizontal element is a clear, round filament with the character of fishing leader. It reveals the random ripple of a triple-ply slit film that is unengaged in the warp. The chainlike vertical is of spun Verel. (Photo by Tom Crane.)

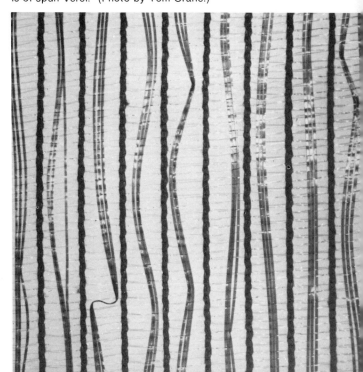

A limited amount of molding and shaping is also possible with certain thermoplastic fibers.

Hydrophobic, in fiber terms, does not imply "fear of water." Rather, it means that a fiber is more or less nonabsorbent. Glass fibers, for instance, are completely nonabsorbent—although glass yarns and cloths, if they are bulky enough, will hold some water. Hydrophobic fibers tend to remain dimensionally stable through changes in humidity and to be quick-drying and resistant to bacteria. They may have so little capacity for absorption or penetration that they are nondyeable.

Hydrophilic denotes the ability of a fiber to absorb water readily. Cellulosics such as cotton and linen are known for their absorbency. Wool will absorb its weight in moisture without feeling damp. Most hydrophilic fibers tend to feel comfortable because the moisture is absorbed and held within the fiber. Bulked hydrophobic fibers may also take up water very rapidly. The effect on comfort, however, is very different. Air trapped within the bulked fiber mass is displaced by water, causing the fabric to feel wet and clammy.

Crimp is the minute waviness of certain natural fibers. Wools, especially the shorter, finer merino fibers spun on the woolen system, have maximum crimp. Crimped fibers are in effect a bed of tiny springs, which fend off abrasion, then bounce back into position. They elongate and flex so successfully that they are a constant inspiration to fiber synthesizers (see below).

Denier designates a numbering system used to measure silk and man-made fibers. The denier number is equal to the weight in grams of nine thousand meters of yarn. The system dates back to early Roman times when a denier was a coin used in buying and selling silk.

Specific gravity or *relative density* refers to weight in relation to bulk. It is pertinent to fibers, yarns, and finished cloths. The desired lightness or heaviness of a finished cloth may be a factor. More often, the factor is cost—yarn yards per pound or cloth ounces in relation to thickness or heft. If, for instance, silk yarns did not have a very low specific gravity—that is, a high yield per pound—silk cloths would be even more costly than they are. Glass filaments have a high specific gravity—almost twice that of silk or wool. For more

bulk in relation to weight, filaments can be texturized or novelty-twisted into a bouclé or loop. Mohair, for instance, has little crimp and a specific gravity similar to wool, but the long, springy fibers are ideally suited for making looped yarns that are light as a feather.

Loft in yarns is the opposite of high specific gravity. What this means is that the fiber mass has a lot of air spun into it. The yarn becomes larger; the cloth, thicker, softer, and seemingly a better value. And if the loft is permanent, as in wool, the fabric is also more resilient.

NATURAL FIBERS

Natural fibers are extracted from inherently fibrous materials found in nature. Natural fibers divide into vegetable, or *cellulosic*, fibers, such as cotton and linen; animal, or *protein*, fibers, such as wool and silk; and a *mineral* fiber, asbestos.

Cellulosic Fibers

Cotton, a seed hair, is relatively durable, absorbent, and comfortable to wear, and the common varieties are inexpensive. The basic fiber types are: *short-staple*, which tends to be dull and fuzzy; *long-staple*, which is often combed into smooth yarns to make broadcloth and cotton gabardine; and *extra-long-staple*, premium cottons such as Egyptian, sea island, and pima. The latter may be nearly as lustrous and almost as expensive as silk. Long-staple cotton yarns may be *carded* and *combed* to lay the fibers parallel. Combed cottons tend to be smoother, more lustrous, and higher in tensile strength. These qualities, plus a greater affinity for dyestuffs, are enhanced by a physical-chemical process called *mercerization*. Today, most cotton cloths that are to be printed or dyed brilliant shades are mercerized. But unless the yarns are of combed long-staple cotton and highly mercerized under tension, they will not take on the characteristic silky sheen.

Since the industrial revolution cotton has dominated the world market. It has been the working fiber for apparel and household use and for institutional and industrial application. In many parts of the world cotton cloth is not only ubiquitous but the chief item in trade.

Description: The cotton fiber during growth is a fine, hollow tube, which, as it matures, collapses and becomes ribbonlike with varying degrees of twist. The length differs with type and grade from half an inch to two and a half inches.

Properties: Cotton has relatively good tensile strength and abrasion resistance; it is absorbent and has a cool hand; it resists sunlight, unless it is sheer; and it releases soil readily.

Qualities: Short-staple cottons, which dominate the market, generally have a mat texture and a dry hand. Long-staple cottons are usually carded and combed to lay the fibers parallel and to produce stronger, more lustrous yarns. Extra-long-staple cotton fibers are smooth, silky, strong, and costly. Because of its dry hand, natural twist, and absorbency, cotton is often blended with man-made fibers.

Bast fibers are removed from the woody stems (linen, jute, ramie, hemp) and swordlike leaves (sisal, piña, abaca) of a wide variety of plants, geographically ranging from the far north to the tropics. The fiber is extracted by *retting* (literally, rotting) the soft, pulpy tissues in woody stems in order to get at the strong, stiffish parallel fibers, or by scraping away the pulpy tissue from swordlike leaves or leaf stalks.

Linen is the most recognizable of bast fibers and the most often used for fabrics.

Description: Linen fibers are retted from the flax plant. Fabrics, especially those from northern Europe, are often sold in an unbleached, natural state referred to as *in the gray*, although the natural color is actually tan. Partial bleaching produces a pearly, *boiled linen*, and single or double bleaching, usually done in the piece, produces a snowy-white opacity.

3-4. Textural richness and variety within one yarn and from one yarn to another is manifested in a solar screen by Marjatta Metsovaara. Two weights of slubby linen are contrasted with a rigid weft of copper wire. The silhouette is spectacular.

Properties: Linen fibers are either *dry-spun* into a lofty, soft yarn or *wet-spun*, which leaves the yarns smoother and more wiry in character, particularly in the gray state. Linen fibers lend body when they are combined with other fibers. This same body permits the weaving of crisp sheers such as theatrical gauze. Draperies of linen sheers may become disappointingly limp and sleazy, however, from humidity or cleaning. Because bast fibers lack resilience, they are susceptible to brittleness in conditions of low humidity, which makes upholstery fabrics even more vulnerable to abrasion. The problem is reduced somewhat by omitting welts, particularly at points of wear such as seat cushions. Linen fibers suffer a second abrasion fault—because printed dyes tend not to penetrate through linen cloths, the color is lost when the topmost fiber wears away. If the cloth is only partially printed, as in a traditional English floral, color abrasion may not present too noticeable a problem. On the other hand, with full-coverage prints—especially those with clear, open color areas—the fault may appear early enough to be a real hazard.

Qualities: Because linen is smooth and highly absorbent, it seems cool. It has long been reputed to be a durable, strong, luxurious fiber. Actually, the reputation is based on *line linen*, an ultra-long-staple variety developed over the centuries as a textile fiber. Line-linen fibers, often ten to thirty inches long, are usually combed and often plied and mercerized. The cloth they produce tends to be hard, durable, smooth, lintfree, and expensive. Today, most linens used in home furnishings are *tow linen*. They are made of short-staple fibers drawn from flax developed for its high yield of linseed oil. Tow linen varies in quality, depending on staple length, and tends in varying degrees to be dull in texture, linty, susceptible to abrasion, and relatively inexpensive. An in-between quality is *demi-line*. Because tow-linen fabrics are dimensionally stable, resistant to sun rot, firm in body, and pleasantly slubbed in texture, they may be ideal as draperies or wall coverings. The chief complaint against linen is its lack of resilience. The resultant wrinkling and crushing can be reduced by a wrinkle-resistant finish, although such finishes are not commonly used in drapery fabrics.

Ramie is said by some to be the fabled "fine linen" of the Bible and the stuff that Egyptian mummy wrappings were made of, so it is rumored to have extraordinary staying power. On the other hand, as it is one of the finest of all natural staple fibers, it is extremely susceptible to abrasion. It serves best as a drapery fabric. Ramie looks nicest as a combed roving with a silky luster.

Hemp fiber ranges from fine to coarse; it may be finer than linen but does not have its luster. It is most frequently used in central Europe and Italy. The Italians combine wet-spun hemp yarns with cotton and sometimes with silk to weave their famous brocatelles. Numerous attempts have been made to use a bleached, dry-spun hemp as a substitute for linen, but to date these efforts have been unsuccessful because of its unavoidable stiffness and weight. In furnishings pure hemp is most often wet-spun to make a theatrical gauze or paper-backed for wall coverings and lampshades. Cable-plied hemp, sometimes called *linen jute*, is a strong and handsome yarn, but it is relatively unknown.

Sisal, to the confusion of all, was formerly known as Manila hemp. In its best grades it has exceptional luster and a lively, wiry spring. Although it dyes brilliantly, color is seldom fast, and even when it is bleached, the white will soon oxidize to the natural ecru. Because the thick, ropy fibers are valuable for industrial uses, it is less available for spinning into a fine yarn. Consequently, sisal seems to be limited in use to carpets, cordage, and art fabrics. With luck we may someday see sisal flat-woven into wall fabrics.

Coir, or coconut fiber, in its best grades is both extremely durable and resistant to disintegration in sunlight or low humidity. Because it is coarse and prickly, its use remains limited to carpets.

Jute, next to linen, is commercially the most important of all bast fibers. The lower grades are used as gunnysacking. Better-grade, long, shimmery fibers are woven into quality burlaps or combined with cottons or other yarns for drapery and upholstery fabrics. Jute is inexpensive, but it does have a few basic drawbacks. It does not resist flexing and abrasion and therefore is limited in use to backings, carpets, wall coverings, or possibly stiffish, rustic draperies. Like sisal, jute has a tendency to lose color and return to the original tan, even when yarns are bleached before dyeing. Often, there is a characteristic odor, which may be problematic in a poorly ventilated room.

Piña, a fine, crisp, grassy fiber from the leaves of the pineapple plant, is beautiful but seldom used in western fabrics. Most piña is woven in the Philippines for use in screens, table mats, and the like.

Grass and *palm* fibers are neither spinnable nor yarns in themselves—facts that limit their use to hand production abroad. But the materials themselves and the woven constructions created with them offer intriguing color and textural variation. Grass and palm fibers are generally used undyed. Their natural colors may mellow: the greens of sea grass, for example, turn into a golden tan.

In addition to the aesthetic uplift given by grass and palm fibers, many provide easily maintained surfaces—often at amazingly low prices. Because most of them suffer from dry heat, they best serve as wall coverings or rigid-wefted window blinds. Some common varieties are listed here.

Madagascar is a palm fiber known as *raffia*. For *lauhala* mats coarse grasses are plaited diagonally into rectangles with four selvages. *Sea grass* is woven into thin mattings and into a thicker, ribbed matting known as *tatami*. Both are excellent wall fabrics. *Grain straw*, *bamboo*, *rattan* and *cane* are all forms of natural vegetation which are woven into various items for furnishings. *Abaca* is a sheer, creamy fiber from the leaves of a tree related to the banana tree.

Protein Fibers

Man-made protein fibers have been produced from such substances as milk solids and vegetable proteins, but for all practical purposes the natural-protein fibers derived from wool fleeces, the soft underhair of certain animals, and fiber from the cocoons of a few Asiatic moths are the most valuable.

3-5. Overtwisting the crepe-spun yarns accounts for the kinky variation within this woolen casement.

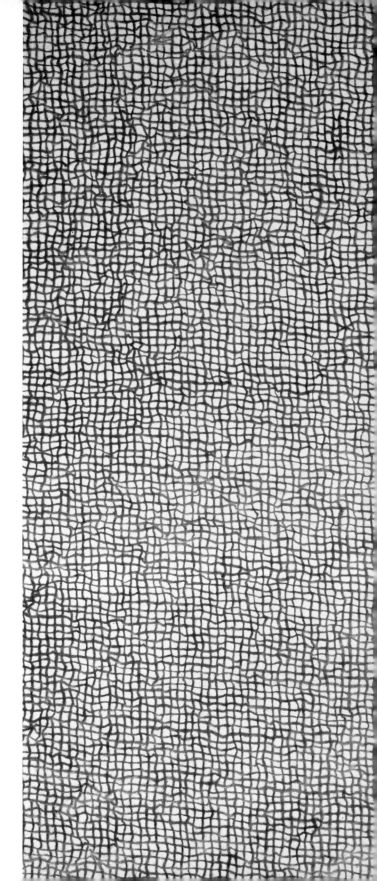

Wool, the dominant protein fiber, is derived from the fleece of a number of types of domesticated sheep. For millennia sheep have been bred for specific climates and end uses, and the many breeds vary not only in diet, endurance, size, and fiber yield, but especially in fiber type. Merino sheep produce quantities of a fine, soft, highly crimped fiber particularly desirable for knits, lightweight fabrics, and soft tweeds. Their relatively short fibers are carded, then spun on the *woolen system* to retain a bulky resilience.

Lincoln, Romney, Cotswold, and cross-bred types are typical long-haired breeds of sheep that yield coarser, straighter, and stronger fibers than merino in lengths averaging from three to five or six inches. These fibers are generally carded, then combed to lay the fibers parallel, then spun on the *worsted system*. Worsteds are smoother yarns than woolens, with high luster and greater tensile strength. In cloths such as gabardine the luster may be exaggerated by singeing or shearing the surface fibers, then polishing the finished cloth with steel calenders.

Description: Wool, a nearly round fiber, is composed of an outer layer of overlapping scales, and the cortex—about ninety percent of the fiber cross section—is composed of bundles of spindle-shaped cells, which give elasticity to the fiber. A third area, the medulla—a network of tiny cells in the center of the shaft—carries the fiber pigment and is rarely visible under a microscope except in coarser fibers. When the medulla is visible in varying proportions to fiber width, it identifies the coarse outer hair present in breeds of sheep supplying good grades of carpet wool.

Wool's natural crimp, or waviness, contributes to its loft and resilience. The barblike epidermal scales cause fibers to cling together, especially when the fiber mass is subjected to heat, moisture, and agitation. The *felting* process, utilized in the production of nonwoven wool felts, is employed in finishing woven cloths to increase compactness, as in meltons, flannels, and coarse homespuns.

Properties: The exceptional resilience of wool is one of its outstanding characteristics. If it is creased or depressed, it literally bounces back, showing no deformation. This quality alone makes wool as desirable for drapery and upholstery as for apparel and carpeting. The spring action not only enhances the wearing quality but self-sustains the original appearance. Wool and other protein fibers are generally resistant to soil and have remarkable soil-releasing properties during cleaning. Because wool is highly absorbent, it has a great affinity for dyestuffs. High-crimp wools—especially lofty yarns spun on the woolen system—have superior insulating properties for both thermal and acoustical control. Like other natural-protein fibers, wool is relatively thermoplastic, so creases, pleats, and embossing tend to be durable.

Wool terms: *Crimp* and *felting* are explained above. *Virgin wool* should designate all-new fiber from the best parts of the fleece, although reliance on known sources is the best guarantee. *Reprocessed* wool is fiber gleaned from waste yarn or fabric scrap which has never been used. *Reused wool* is recycled from used wool fabrics or rags. *Noils* are very short wool fibers and waste. *In the grease* indicates fabrics in which the natural lanolin has not been extracted; it is scoured out in finishing. The *Wool Mark* represents one-hundred-percent-pure virgin wool that has been approved by the Wool Bureau. Wool Mark fabrics are available from processors who follow guidelines set by the Wool Bureau. (For further information write the Wool Bureau, 919 Third Avenue, New York, N.Y. 10017.)

Mohair fiber is long (up to twelve or eighteen inches), smoother than wool, and available in fine to coarse diameters. Mohair is unusually springy, translucent, and lustrous. Like wool, it has a natural affinity for dye. Its wrinkle resistance, lively hand, and an aptitude for cleaning justify the high initial cost. Mohair can be successfully blended with other fibers. Next to wool and silk, this long, silky fleece from the Angora goat (native to Asia Minor) is the protein fiber most frequently used in furnishings. Its body, luster, translucency, and natural resistance to soil make it one of the finest yarns for casements. Mohair, especially *kid mohair* taken from the first shearing, makes the finest upholstery plush.

Cashmere is the fine, downy underhair of the Kashmir goat (native to the Himalayan highlands).

It is so delicate and costly that, with the exception of using it as a luxurious chaise throw, it is hard to justify the cost in home furnishings.

Common *goat hair* is so coarse and scratchy that it is used only in some flat tribal rugs. Gray goat fibers blended with other softer fibers to facilitate spinning are most often used in tailors' canvas or to give body and surface interest to casement fabrics and printed cloths.

Camel's hair, like cashmere, is a downy underhair, generally too susceptible to abrasion and too costly for upholstery. When this soft hair is blended with the outer, prickly guard hairs, it produces a superior yarn for casements. The various Andean members of the camel family—*vicuña*, *alpaca,* and *llama*—also yield valuable fiber. For its beauty, fineness, and cost alpaca ranks high as a luxury furnishings fabric. Its soft luster, silky hand, and natural colors, which range from white and beige through rust and brown to gray and black, are remarkable indeed.

Horsehair, which resists soil and wear, is mostly woven in France. By necessity it is woven in narrow widths, and it has become increasingly expensive. There is still a revered place in the furnishings field for horsehair upholstery.

Silk encompasses a broad family of related protein fibers spun by various oriental silk moths. The utilization of silk as a textile fiber, beginning with the dawn of Chinese civilization, has always been synonymous with luxury, and because sericulture—the art of producing raw-silk filaments from the cocoons of silkworms—requires intensive labor, silk prices are still skyrocketing today. Japan, formerly the chief exporter of silk yarns, is today a principal importer because labor costs there are no longer competitive. Most silk fabrics are now woven in China, Japan, Korea, India, Thailand, France, and Italy. Depending on the type of moth, its diet, and how it is processed, the range of yarn and even fabric types is very wide. There is a great difference between *cultivated silk*, spun by worms fed on mulberry leaves and reeled from their cocoons in continuous filaments before the maturing moths escape, and the various *wild silks*, spun by worms that feed on oak leaves. Because wild-silk filaments have been broken by the evacuating moths before the cocoons are gathered, the broken filaments are spun into yarns in the same manner as other staple fibers.

Description: The very fine protein fiber extruded as a continuous filament is straight, strong, and lustrous. The natural color of cultivated silk is milk white, while wild silks are cream to medium brown. The beauty of wild silks is highly prized, and these fibers are seldom dyed.

Silk terms: *Reeled silk* refers to the continuous filaments reeled from the cocoons of cultivated silkworms, and it averages one thousand feet in length. To make a heavier yarn, filaments from two or more cocoons may be reeled together. *Douppioni silk* is reeled from two cocoons that have grown together. The occasional meshing of filaments from the two worms causes characteristic slubs to form. Shantung is a typical douppioni cloth. *Spun silk* is silk recovered from pierced cocoons or portions of cocoons that cannot be reeled. All wild silks are spun; *tussah* is one of the best known, from which the traditional *pongee* and *honan* are woven. Cultivated-silk cocoons, from which moths must escape to perpetuate the life cycle, are also valuable sources of spun silk, from which white and most dyed, textured silk cloths are fabricated. *Noil silk*, or *bourette*, is spun from very short silk fibers—often waste. Typical cloths are soft and nubby with dark flecks of chrysalis. *Raw silk* means *in the gum*, or stiff with a natural serecin coating, which is normally boiled off either in the yarn state or in piece-goods finishing. *Raw silk* is never used in the west, but spun silk is often wrongly called by this term. *Weighted silk* was silk given weight and body by immersing it in adulterating agents. Fortunately, this practice is obsolete. The Pure Silk label precludes weighting.

MAN-MADE FIBERS

Although fibers can be categorized in several ways, the basic distinction is between those provided by nature and those that are *man-made*. Man-made fibers are extruded as filaments by forcing a fiber-forming substance through a minute nozzle called a *spinneret*. Extruded filaments may be single, or *monofilament*, such as nylon fishing line. More often, filaments are extruded in groups or bundles known as *multifilaments*. Neither monofilaments nor multifilaments are spun—they are in themselves yarns or yarn components. The general characteristics of man-made fibers are given in Chart 1, and more specific information is availble

in publications listed in the Bibliography.

Man-made filaments may be conditioned in a variety of ways. Often they are *texturized*, or *bulked*, that is, given a permanent crimp or curl to make a lofty, resilient, more "natural" yarn. This "permanent wave," which gives resilience, bulk without weight, and a softer hand, is the result of several processes, of which Banlon, Tycora (trade names of yarn converters), and Cumuloft (trade name of a fiber producer) are typical (see figure 3-6). These texturized or bulked yarns save the expense of processing and spinning a yarn from masses of short or staple fibers (see figure 3-2). Texturized filaments tend to resist pilling but may be susceptible to snagging.

3-6. To make man-made fibers, a chemical solution is extruded through a spinneret, which resembles a miniature shower head. This Acrilan acrylic is extruded into a water bath. Other fibers are air-borne. (Photo courtesy Monsanto Chemical Company.)

"Natural" Fibers

Man-made fibers extruded directly from natural solutions include *fiberglass* (from glass), *latex* (from rubber), and wirelike *metallics* (from metal). Most metallic yarns, however, are not extruded but made as slit films (see Part 3, section 4).

Cellulosic Fibers

Cellulosic fiber extracted from such woody vegetable material as cotton linter and wood pulp may be *regenerated* to form rayon or *reconstituted* to form acetate and triacetate. *Rayon*, which is almost pure cellulose, is the oldest man-made fiber (1910). Most rayon is *viscose rayon*. Other forms are *high wet modulus rayon*, which has greater stability in washing; *cuprammonium rayon*, a fine, quality fiber mostly used in apparel; and *saponified rayon*, which is reconverted from acetate filaments to obtain fiber that dyes likes rayon. *High-tenacity rayons* are modified to achieve better dimensional stability and resistance to light.

    Acetate, which is extruded from cellulose acetate, requires special dyes. This dye selectivity makes it useful in cross-dyeing. *Triacetate* is a modified form of acetate that contains a higher ratio of acetate to cellulose and resists machine washing and high temperatures better.

Synthetic Fibers

The term *synthetic* refers to man-made fibers that are not derived from natural substances. Sometimes referred to as noncellulosic fibers, they are synthesized primarily from petrochemicals. Their fiber-forming substances are *long-chain polymers*, chains of like units of simple chemicals linked together end-to-end. Stretching or drawing after extrusion permits the molecules within the filaments to be arranged in an ordered pattern. In general, synthetic fibers are thermoplastic, nonabsorbent, smooth, nonporous, nonallergenic, and impervious to moths and mildew.

In addition to the original generic fibers, referred to as the *first generation*, newer modifications have been introduced to change both physical appearance and performance. Variations in crimp, strength, cross section, luster, dyeability, flame resistance, and static propensities have created a *second generation* of man-made fibers. They can usually be solution-dyed, high-shrunk, deep-dyed, or texturized. The *third generation* of man-made fibers offers soil-retardant properties, antistatic finishes, and more sophisticated textured filaments for specific end uses. *Bicomponent* and *biconstituent* fibers have been introduced—fibers composed of two elements with slightly different characteristics—with increased bulk and resilience. New generic fibers, aramid and novolid, have been added. Nomex, an aramid-based fiber first introduced by Du Pont as a modified nylon, has low flammability ratings and no melting point. Konol, a novolid fiber, is also flame-resistant and non-melting, but at present it is not available for furnishings.

Blends

For reasons of appearance, hand, endurance, and economy, *blends* of man-made fibers and of man-made and natural fibers continue to develop. An *intimate blend* consists of fibers spun together within the same yarn ply. Two or more different filaments twisted together are called *combination filament yarns*.

CHART 1. PRINCIPAL MAN-MADE FIBERS.

Regenerated Cellulosic Fibers			Mineral Fibers	Synthetic Long-chain Polymers
rayon	acetate	triacetate	glass	nylon

viscose rayon
  Avril (FMC)
  Jetspun (American Enka)
  Enkrome (American Enka)
  Coloray (Courtaulds)
  Fibro (Courtaulds)
high wet modulus rayon
  Zantrel (American Enka)
cuprammonium rayon
  Bemberg (Beaunit)
	Estron (Eastman)
	
	Celanese (Celanese)
	
	Acele (Du Pont)
		Arnel (Celanese)
		Tricel (Courtaulds)
		Rhonel (Rhône-Poulenc)
			Fiberglass (Owens-Corning)
			Beta (Owens-Corning)
			PPG (Pittsburgh Plate Glass)
				Antron (Du Pont)
				Antron III (Du Pont)
				Caprolan (Allied Chemical)
				Perlon (Bayer)
				Nomex (Du Pont)
				Qiana (Du Pont)
				Cadon (Monsanto)
				Cumuloft (Monsanto)

Plus

low cost wide range of types, deniers, and lusters easy to dye	low cost light-resistant dimensionally stable low static electricity fair absorbency flame-retardant (Acele)	same as acetate	light-resistant low cost dimensionally stable fireproof drip-dry	abrasion-resistant high tensile strength resilient antistatic (Antron, Cadon)

Minus

poor light resistance
low stability
variable abrasion
  resistance
low resilience
	low abrasion resistance
	heat-sensitive
		same as acetate	low abrasion resistance
			undyeable
			laundering·requires special care
				collects static electricity
				  and soil
				low light resistance
				spun yarns tend to pill

modacrylic	acrylic	saran	polyester	olefin
Dynel (Union Carbide)	Acrilan (Monsanto)	Enjay (Eastman)	Dacron (Du Pont)	Durel (Celanese)
Verel (Eastman)	Creslan (American Cyanamid)		Fortrel (Celanese)	Meraklon
Kanekalon (Kanekafuchi)	Orlon (Du Pont)		Kodel (Eastman)	Herculon (Hercules)
	Zefran (Dow Badische)		Vycron (Beaunit)	Polypropylene (Thiokol)
Leavil	Dralon (Bayer)		Tergal (Rhodiaceta)	
	Dolan (Hoechst)		Terital	
	Leacril		Terylene (ICI)	
			Trevira (Hystron)	
			Textura (Rohm & Haas)	
			Diolen	

modacrylic	acrylic	saran	polyester	olefin
flame-resistant	light-resistant	lightfast	light-resistant	low cost
light resistant	dimensionally stable	colorfast	permanent body	mildew-resistant
bulky	bulky	weather-resistant	dimensionally stable	nonabsorbent
		flame-resistant	wrinkle-resistant	stain-resistant
		soil-resistant	abrasion-resistant	lightweight
				resilient

modacrylic	acrylic	saran	polyester	olefin
low melting point	modest abrasion resistance in flat fabrics	heat-sensitive	spun yarns tend to pill	heat-sensitive
low abrasion resistance for upholstery	cannot be made flame-retardant (at present)	heavy	stains hard to remove	hard to dye
			collects static electricity	tends to pill
				collects static electricity

3. Yarns

Yarn, as opposed to *thread*, the sewing medium, is a general term for the linear materials employed in fabric construction. These materials may be natural, man-made, or synthetic fibers or—in the broadest sense—grass, wire, ribbon, or rope.

MONOFILAMENTS

The simplest kind of yarn has one indivisible component—a *monofilament*—such as a strand of horsehair. Man-made monofilaments include plastic yarns resembling fishline, ribbonlike synthetic raffias, twisted papers, and flat slit films such as Mylar and Lurex. Man-made monofilaments are among the newest of yarn types, offering aesthetic and practical possibilities not found in fibrous yarns (see figures 2-2 and 3-36).

MULTIFILAMENTS

When several filaments are carried as one yarn, the yarn is called a *multifilament*. Multifilaments can be twisted or plied for a variety of effects. Both monofilaments and multifilaments are more direct and less expensive than spinning staple fibers into a yarn (see Part 3, section 2). They possess more

tensile strength and have a natural resistance to pilling, although they are susceptible to snagging.

SPUN YARNS

Today, the majority of yarns are still spun from either natural-fiber staple such as cotton and wool or from man-made multifilaments cut into short lengths. Yarn is generally spun by one of the original systems developed for natural fibers—the cotton system, the linen system, the woolen system, or the worsted system. As each system retains its own *yarn count*, or size, the only universal measure is in terms of yards per pound. (U.S. conversion to the metric system will simplify this outdated measure.)

YARN TWISTS

After drawing and spinning, yarns are twisted to increase strength and reduce susceptibility to abrasion. A yarn before it is drawn and twisted is called a *roving*. A slightly twisted, or *slack-twisted*, yarn exposes its silky fibers, while a very tightly twisted, or *crepe-spun*, yarn becomes pebbly, elastic, and mat-textured. Most twisting falls somewhere in between. The twisting direction is normally clockwise—i.e., it has an *s-twist*. For certain novelty effects a *z-twist*—counterclockwise—may be used in combination with an s-twist.

PLIED YARNS

After twisting, all yarns are still one-ply, or *singles*. The coarser sizes of single yarns may have the advantage of expressing their fiber content—appearing irregular or random. Singles, however, have neither the tensile strength nor the abrasion resistance of *plied* yarns—those in which two or more yarns or strands are twisted together. Two or three plies are common. Four are not uncommon, but practically all yarn is one- or two-ply. Twisting multiple plies produce a round, *cable-plied* yarn. An untwisted multiple-ply yarn is referred to as a *floss*. Yarns with plies of two or more colors are spoken of as *marled*; when they are used in a carpet or pile fabric, a random pattern called *moresque* is produced.

3-7. From top to bottom: one-ply, or singles, yarn, in this case with a natural slub; two-ply yarn; three-ply, round yarn; multiple, or cable-ply yarn, which is round and cordlike.

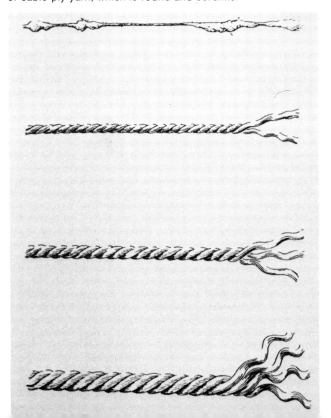

A *slub* yarn—slightly random in diameter and profile—may be a natural result of spinning uncombed fibers, as in slubby linens or woolen tweeds. Slubs may also be induced mechanically, but the mechanical repeats tend to cause occasional, unwanted patterns within the goods. This is even more true with the exaggerated slubs of flame yarns.

A *nub* was originally a random clot of short, dense fibers incorporated into the yarn during spinning. In most cloths it is picked out in the finishing. If nubs are frequent enough, they may be left in to become part of the cloth's textural character. Nubs may be purposefully added to woolens during spinning. Too often, however, these nubs do not dye evenly with the finished cloth. They are occasionally dyed in contrasting colors before spinning, as in a Donegal tweed. In either case they are apt to appear foreign and busy—*on* but not *of* the goods.

NOVELTY YARNS

A *ratiné* is made by twisting one heavy ply back and forth, like rickrack, across a threadlike core. A variant of ratiné, called *bouclé*, appears looped or curly; yet another variation has intermittent *seeds* or *knots*.

Yarns may also be knit or braided. Pilelike *chenille* yarns are woven, then cut into ribbons between the spaced warp ends, forming small fringes that become round in section when they are washed and finished. A new chenillelike yarn is a synthetic ratiné that has been abraded to cut and raise the fibers into a feathery, high-bulk "chenille." These feathery and flocked chenilles are inexpensive in comparison to woven yarns.

A *gimp* is one yarn, usually a silk or metallic spiral, which is wrapped closely around a central core to cover it completely. Elastic yarns are usually a gimp with a latex core.

Yarns such as *eiderdown* are made of felted-wool roving. Other yarns are *space-dyed* by dipping parts of a long skein into different-color dyes. *Printed yarns* are more common today. They are sometimes splotched with a whole spectrum of color but seldom to good effect.

Synthetic monofilament.

Slit-film laminate of aluminum sandwiched between polyester.

Raffialike crushed slit film of high-luster viscose.

Texturized multifilament.

Two strands of bulked multifilament stretch yarn.

Eiderdown, a felted roving.

Floss of several strands of slub singles.

Hand-spun mohair with a characteristic burst of open fibers.

Hand-spun two-ply woolen yarn.

Berber yarn, a slubby, heathered machine-spun singles.

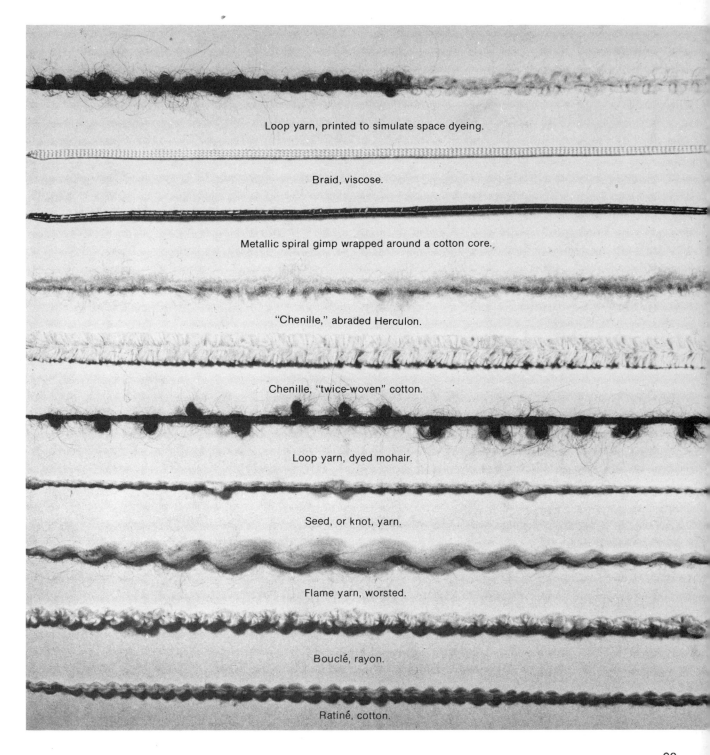

Loop yarn, printed to simulate space dyeing.

Braid, viscose.

Metallic spiral gimp wrapped around a cotton core.

"Chenille," abraded Herculon.

Chenille, "twice-woven" cotton.

Loop yarn, dyed mohair.

Seed, or knot, yarn.

Flame yarn, worsted.

Bouclé, rayon.

Ratiné, cotton.

STRETCH YARNS

Yarns with durable, springy elongation and return range from true elastic gimps of yarn wrapped around a core of spandex or latex to the newer array of stretch yarns in which a multifilament yarn is texturized by heat-setting a springlike coil in the filament. These yarns, certainly among the best for stretch upholstery, create a durable stretch with a core of as little as two percent monofilament spandex or Lycra. The general degree of overall stretch required is between fourteen and seventeen percent (see Part 2, section 2).

HAND-SPUN YARNS

Slow and laborious, the hand-spinning process may require a week to card, spin, ply, and scour enough yarn for a single yard of fabric. At their best, however, fabrics made of hand-spun yarns are not only beautiful in themselves but embody very special variations of color and texture—appropriate and timely antidotes to the monotonous surfaces of today's interiors. Here is organic texture, reminiscent of the random variations in grass, bark, and sand—in short, the out-of-doors ingredients that are missing indoors in suburbs and cities. With a rusticity that is not phony or artificial, these cloths, more than any other furnishing ingredient, fill a psychic and aesthetic void.

It is easy to argue that from the point of view of fabric, the real loss of the industrial revolution was not hand weaving but hand spinning, for the power loom can and does duplicate hand-woven fabrics very well. The lively variations and gradations, changes of pace, and "mistakes" associated with the hand-weaving tradition are more apt to derive from the yarn than the loom.

Hand-spun yarns, available today in luxury fabrics, are apt to be in coarser counts, most often of wool, which are suitable for simple cloths or carpets that exploit their textural richness. The variations come partly from irregularities in the spinning itself, such as abrupt variations in thickness and modulation of slack or crepe twist. But very often the "flavor" derives from spinning ungraded and unhomogenized fibers. The variations of fiber length, crimp, and color dominate. They also influence the profile of the spun yarns. Permutations caused by hand dyeing are also a factor. The importance of hand spinning far outdistances its small, luxury market. It sets a standard, educates the eye and hand, and points up the need to achieve humanizing relief in other materials, such as the thoroughly plastic fabric shown in figure 3-4.

Of course, variations in machine-spun yarns are possible, but we are still suffering from the century-long drive toward standardization. To eliminate flaws and achieve uniformity, producer and consumer have accepted yarns—and fabrics—as bland as refined sugar.

Perhaps there is a lesson in the lively hand of Mexican cotton. This yarn is not hand-spun but produced on old-fashioned commercial frames that were sold off by the English years ago because they yielded a "low-quality" product. Another example is the original Berber yarn developed by Tisca of Switzerland. The aim was to synthesize the hand spinning of North Africa, but the achievement was the production, both by hand and by machine, of dramatically beautiful blends of natural fibers—often without precedent. Now much imitated, these yarns undoubtedly point to a reversal in spinning's long evolution away from organic expression (see figures 1-5, 2-9, and 3-8).

3-10. Hand-spun wools provide an organic, barklike texture in this Moroccan fabric. The knots and slubs, the random thick-and-thin silhouette, and the graduated color that results from blending ungraded fiber are exaggerated by freely mixing a dark and a light yarn. Fabric by Margit Pinter.

→

C-1. Fabric color can be the most splendid in the man-made world. Its iridescence may rival that of flowers, feathers, or minerals. *Landis*, a twill-woven double cloth, is based on six graduated colors, which cross each other to produce a total of twenty-five shades against an inky matrix. Designed by Richard Landis and Jack Lenor Larsen.

C-2. For a relaxation and sleeping mezzanine opening on a large, high-ceilinged living area, the objectives were to please the senses and to support the psyche, or—put differently—to intensify the quality of life and to create a haven for quiet hours far removed from daytime cares. A broad range of fabrics and theatrical techniques are employed. Together with light controls, the two layers of printed sheer perform as theatrical scrims. Together with an opaque, sound-deadening curtain, the three layers allow for: (1) total separation of the two areas, (2) total openness to maximize space and lengthen vista, and (3) varying degrees of translucency, in which each area borrows space from the others. The carpet, which is so exaggerated in texture and pale color that it would be impractical in work areas, is, here, a delight to bare feet. The wall fabric is a satiny, slubby warp laminate. Layers of fabric blinds at the window, a filtered skylight overhead, sophisticated lighting controls, and low, peripheral up-lighting allow for amplification of or substitution for morning sun and for turning on serene, romantic, or celestial moods in the evening. The fabric walls are washed with light from below, which flatters both the space and its occupants. The patterns and textures evoke a gardenlike setting. The pink-cloud coloring can be grayed or heightened by admixtures of colored light. Designed by Jack Larsen and Charles Forberg for Visiona 4, Frankfurt, 1974, sponsored by Bayer Chemical Company.

4. Constructions

NO-ELEMENT FABRICS

Felts

The original *felts* were made of wool and other animal fibers that were not taken to yarn form but instead intermeshed by heat, moisture, and agitation. Cellulosic and synthetic felts require the addition of an adhesive or bonding agent.

Knitted or woven cloths of woolen fibers can be shrunk to such an extent that their structures are submerged into a felted structure that has greater tensile strength than a plain felt.

To provide tensile strength in felts other than wool, supported felts have a woven or nonwoven scrim sandwiched between two layers of matted fiber.

Nonwoven Fabrics

The term *nonwoven* is misleading and is not to be confused with knits, laces, or other *not* woven fabrics with one or more yarn elements. In nonwoven fabrics not only is the weaving process dispensed with, but the yarn phase is also omitted. Nonwovens, as opposed to films, are fibrous. Indeed, they are often feltlike mats created with man-made fibers. A bonding agent of some sort may be necessary for adhesion.

As in nonwoven viscose ribbons, the fibers may be *unidirectional*—more or less parallel—or laid in a directionless web. More frequently, nonwovens are made by the *wet-process*, or papermaking, method, in which fibers are suspended in water and deposited on a sievelike screen. They may also be made by the *dry-process* method, in which bats of loose fiber are compressed with heat and an adhesive material. This is called a *bonded web*.

Disposable nonwovens are usually made of rayon or cotton waste, while durable nonwovens may be made with any number of fibers. Either may be supported for strength. Heavier qualities, including carpets, are needle-punched. *Needle punching* is a unique process in that it is mechanical rather than relying on heat, pressure, and adhesives. Hundreds of barbed hooks pass up and down through a web of staple fibers. The entangling fibers themselves become the "stiching" element.

Spun-bonded nonwovens are made from continuous thermoplastic filaments that are laid in a directionless mass, then welded with heat.

To date, one characteristic of nonwoven fabrics is dimensional stability, or—stated negatively—lack of flexibility. Not only is the elasticity we expect to find in twisted yarns missing in non-woven fabrics, but the basic structure employed is rigidly set in an unshifting, triangular pattern. Unlike the rectangles formed by yarn crossings in woven fabrics or the soft loops in knitted fabrics—either of which will compress or elongate under tension—the triangle is so stubbornly unmoving that it produces a more or less rigid cloth. For a fabric used as a substrate, laminate, reinforcement, or for molding under heat and pressure, this stability is a plus. It is even acceptable in certain types of window fabric. But the springy, conforming fit we find so desirable in cushioning and apparel fabrics is lacking so far in nonwoven fabrics.

Films

Films are nonfibrous, no-element man-made fabrics. They are most often made from solutions of acetate, PVC, or polyester. Because films are dense—they lack the lofty air spaces of fibrous fabrics—they consume a maximum of material per millimeter of thickness. For this reason they tend to be thin. Their smooth surfaces tend to be abrasion- and soil-resistant, waterproof, unbreathing, and monotonous. While embossing and printing can reduce this monotony, these processes are often so imitative in character that the results appear unconvincing, if not phony. The practice of laminating film over fabric—or fabric over film (see Part 3, section 6)—not only lends support and resilience but improved hand and better texture.

Films can also be *slit* into ribbonlike yarns. The most common are the metallics, in which films of acetate or polyester are laminated to both sides of a thin layer of aluminum, then slit to the desired width. Other slit films, as shown in figure 3-36, are used "straight" or folded into a ribbon.

Foams

Like films, *foams* (in roll-goods form) are man-made no-element fabrics. They are "industrial" rather than furnishings fabrics because, to date, they have been used entirely as substrates.

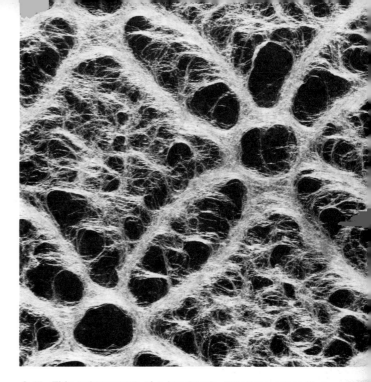

3-11. This enlargement of a handmade Japanese paper illustrates how fibers are laid down in wet-process fabrics. This very special fabric also demonstrates the potential for beauty in industrial nonwovens.

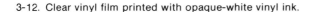

3-12. Clear vinyl film printed with opaque-white vinyl ink.

Whether they are bonded to the back of a face cloth or used as a pad or batting, the tiny, air-filled cells of foam are useful in lending bulk and softness or thermal and acoustical insulation. Unsupported, their tear strength is exceptionally low. Too many of them disintegrate with heat, light, or simply age.

Extruded Fabrics

The relatively new *extruded fabrics* are related to films in that they are nonfibrous and made directly from a solution. Unlike films, their surface tends to be pierced and varied. Resilience makes even shaping possible. One of the earliest, Du Pont's Vexar, used for packing fruit and covering chimneys of café candles, points up a potential future. A more recent development from England (figure 3-13) is the prototype for a handsome, exceedingly inexpensive window fabric.

SINGLE-ELEMENT FABRICS

In contrast to some no-element fabrics, fabrics constructed with yarn elements tend to be fibrous in content, and, depending on the size or the count of the yarns, the structure is visible enough to be a prime factor in their aesthetic appeal.

Like felt, single-element techniques were developed in most cultures before weaving. They may be an outgrowth of basketry and plaiting or a simultaneous development. When looms were invented to produce a more uniform cloth faster, some of the single-element techniques such as looping and plaiting fell out of common usage. The fact that weaving was industrialized while single-element techniques were not widened the breach. Some of these old fabric forms may yet figure in postindustrial monolithic fabric structures.

Single-element fabrics in current use are jersey knits, crochets, and some laces. Their use in furnishings is still limited. The extremely elastic resilience of knit fabrics has generally been considered a liability, not an asset, for upholstery. At some future date when upholstery coverings are full-fashioned and have the potential for quick change and immersion cleaning, knits will come into their own.

3-13. Extruded fabric is filmlike and slightly "embossed." The pierced grill pattern provides both stability and a draping quality. Variations in the threadlike web relieve monotony.

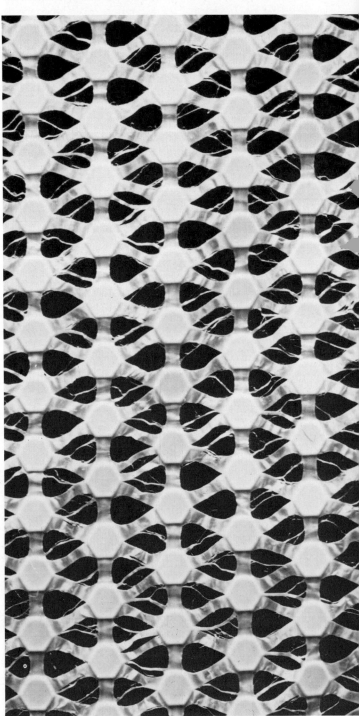

TWO-ELEMENT WEAVES

Two-element weaves dominate the market, both in quantity of production and in number of variations. Of all woven fabrics, the majority have only two elements. (There is a discussion of two-element fabrics other than weaves at the end of this section.)

Weaving remains the type of construction by which most cloth is produced. Because it is so ubiquitous, some explanation of pertinent terminology is required here.

Weaving itself is the right-angle interlacing of two or more elements. If these elements are yarn (rigid materials such as wire may also be woven), the plane produced is pliable. The *warp* is the set (or sets) of yarns that runs along the length of the fabric. These yarns are strung onto the loom, usually feeding off a cylinder called a *warp beam*.

The *filling*, or *weft* (*woof* in archaic Anglo-Saxon), is the yarn that interlaces through the warp (most often in a boatlike *shuttle*) to form the cloth. The *loom* is the apparatus (figure 3-14) on which cloth is woven. A loom has *harnesses*, which raise or lower the warp in a predetermined pattern.

Between the harnesses and the woven cloth the *beater*, or *batten*, holds a comb, or *reed*. Its fineness determines the closeness of the warp yarns. The beater pushes each *shot*, or *pick*, of filling into the cloth at a controllable density. The woven cloth is rolled onto the *cloth beam* at the front of the loom. This beam holds a *piece* of cloth, usually forty to a hundred yarns long.

All looms, whether a narrow ribbon or a wide carpet is being woven, are essentially the same. A power loom is basically a hand loom with motors and controls that do the work. On a *fly-shuttle* loom the shuttle is not thrown by hand but shot through by pulling a cord. Because of this semi-mechanization, fly-shuttle fabrics are technically termed *hand-loomed*, not hand-woven. *Shuttleless* looms are a recent development. They produce faster than other power looms and easily combine up to eight filling yarns, but the cloth is no better. In fact, it lacks the characteristic and sometimes useful *selvage*, or self-edge, of woven cloth.

3-14. This diagram of a simple four-harness hand loom illustrates the basic process by which all woven fabrics are made. At the rear (right) hundreds of parallel warp yarns roll off the cylindrical warp beam; over a back beam; through a tensioning device that also keeps the yarns in sequence; through needlelike heddles in harness frames that control the weave patterns; and, with one shot—or pick—of weft yarn, the shuttle passes through the triangular opening (called the shed) between the upper and lower yarns. Each pick is pushed into the new cloth by a comb-like reed in a hinged beater. The woven fabric will roll over the front beam and onto the cloth beam below.

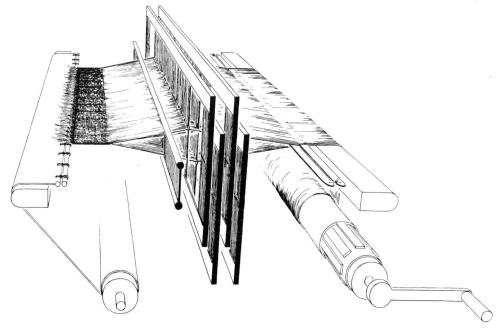

Looms may have additional controls, or *attachments*. The most common and the most useful are the *dobby* and *jacquard* attachments, which, like a player piano, determine the patterning of the weave. A dobby attachment, used on a harness loom, is limited to relatively simple, often geometric patterns such as figure 2-6. Because the jacquard attachment controls each warp end individually and is more complex, it can maneuver finely drawn *patterns* such as florals.

All woven fabrics are based on one of three constructions: plain weave, twill weave, and satin weave. The extraordinary variety of cloth that can be produced is brought about by the interrelationship of weave, weight and density, fiber and yarn, and color effects such as striping. The major variations and derivatives are shown in Chart 2.

Plain Weave

Of all textile constructions, *plain*, or *taffeta*, weave is the most universal. It is the foundation of hundreds of cloths in all fibers and for every use—sieves and filters for industry, gauzes for medicine, steel blasting mats (which weigh a ton), and the sheerest of chiffons. Plain weave and its derivatives are also a basic stuff of all furnishing fabrics from burlap to chintz, from plush to carpeting.

The simplest variation, which applies to all weaves, is *grouping*, or carrying two or more yarns as one. For instance, doubled yarns in warp and weft produce basket weave. Two, three, or more ends of cotton in each direction produce monk's cloth. Mixing yarn sizes will induce similar effects, e.g., two warp ends of plied yarns crossed with a heavier singles weft produce quality canvas, duck, or sailcloth. The singles weft absorbs more moisture and swelling and tightens the weave.

Density is the most direct modifier of weaves. When you consider that approximately the same count of cotton yarn is used in the plain-woven constructions of cheesecloth, muslin, and canvas, the importance of density becomes clearer. As progressive density increases both fiber weight and production time, it becomes a key factor in fabric cost.

3-15. Looms with a jacquard attachment are capable of weaving very complex patterns with long repeats. Marga Hiele-Vatter's famous *Parquet* is shown here on the reverse side to better illustrate the order of interlacing.

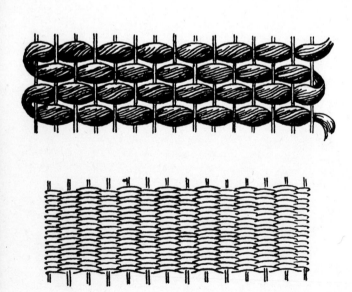

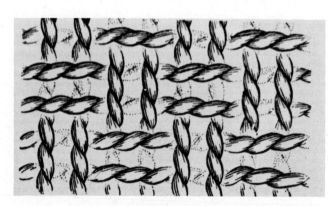

3-16. Two variations of filling-face plain weave. In the upper sketch the count of warp and weft is the same, but yarn sizes are unequal. In the lower version yarn sizes are equal, but the spacing is not. A definite vertical rib will result.

3-17. Two variations of plain weave. The top sketch shows rib weave, in which the weft is normally crammed to make a rib, as in figure 3-16. Basket weave, shown at bottom, is normally a balanced cloth in which equal numbers of warp and weft yarns are woven as one.

CHART 2. CLASSIFICATION OF FABRIC STRUCTURES.

Construction	Nonwoven	Cloths	Plain Weave	Cloths
No-element without fibers	foams films			
	unsupported	Pliofilm shower curtaining		
	supported	Naugahyde		

	laminated	metallic ribbon
		  Mylar
		  Lurex		

	extruded fabrics	Vexar		
with fibers	felts			
	unsupported	felt paper		
	supported bondeds	net-based felt		
	unsupported	Pellon		
	supported	stitch-bondeds		
	spun-bonded	Reemay Pellon Typar Tyvek Cerex		
	needle-punched fabrics	Ozite		
Single-element	crochet knits	tubular jersey flat-bed knits		
	weft knits	fishnets tricot Milanese		
	warp knits	fishnets filet lace		
	nets	bobbin lace soutache braided rugs		
	plaiting sprang macramé looping knotless nets			
Two-element			float weave	barathea crepe bark cloth pique huckaback waffle weave honeycomb lace weave mock leno

Construction	Nonwoven	Cloths	Plain Weave	Cloths
Two-element (cont'd.)			balanced plain weave (one-and-one)	organdy muslin gingham
	laces	nottingham lace bobbinet		monk's cloth
	warp knits	Rachel knits Sabego double knits	basket weave (two-and-two)	hopsacking canvas duck
	twining gauze		half-basket (two-and-one)	sailcloth
compound cloths	bondeds laminates embroidery tufting quilting		rib weave	faille taffeta grosgrain ottoman
			leno tapestry	marquisette Göbelin kilim
Three-element	Malimo double knits laminates		brocade* warp filling continuous discontinuous	"tapestry" weave** brocade** lappet swivel dotted swiss
			pile weaves warp-pile cut	velvet** velour** plush frieze**
			uncut	grospoint terrycloth** velveteen
			filling-pile	corduroy
Four-element	Malimo double knits laminates		double plain weave	matelassé*** Finn weave double cloths
			double brocade***	

Twill Weave	Cloths	Satin Weave	Cloths
balanced twill (two-and-two)	cheviot	warp-face	satin
	houndstooth	filling-face	sateen
warp face	herringbone		antique satin
	drill	warp-and-filling-face	damask**
	denim	single	
filling-face	gabardine	double	
warp-and-filling-face	twill tapestry		
reverse twill	twill damask		
	diaper		
	bird's-eye		
fancy twills	diamond		

	brocaded cloths*		brocatelle**
	matelassé***		
	brocatelle***		
	velvet		

double twill weave		*three-element cloths may be combined with a base of plain, twill, satin, or any combination of these **often woven with a jacquard attachment	

Balanced plain weave.

Rib weave.

Crammed rib weave.

Basket weave.

Left-hand balanced twill.

Like gingham and muslin, most plain weaves are more or less *balanced*, i.e., they have an equal yarn count in warp and weft. By *cramming* extra yarns in one direction, a rib is formed. Rep, faille, taffeta, poplin, grosgrain, and ottoman are typical plain weaves with crammed warps. Cramming the weft is more typical in primitive cloths and in heavier weights. The same technique, with less desirable results, may be used to throw bulky novelty yarns to the face of some upholstery cloths—often a negative factor in wear, especially when, for reasons of economy in mass production, fine yarns make up the warp. (It should be added that twill and satin structures may also be employed for this purpose.) Cramming wefts on strong warps is the usual construction of blankets, tapestries, and flat-woven rugs (figure 3-17). A fine warp with a heavier weft is typical of such handsome cloths as Thai silk.

Leno, a unique variation on plain weave, is actually a weaving technique, not a weave. Here, pairs of warp cross between insertions of weft. In a sheer fabric a leno produces a firmer cloth than a plain weave, and the incidence of slippage is reduced. Fancy lenos sometimes involve three or more warp ends, a complex filling arrangement, or a spaced warp. As illustrated in figure 3-21, blocks of leno may also be combined with other weaves on dobby or jacquard looms.

Tapestry, another important derivative of plain weave, usually with a crammed weft, is not to be confused with wall hangings or tapestry weave (a type of jacquard upholstery cloth shown in figure 3-34). It is a hand technique of joining discontinuous wefts in order to achieve contiguous areas of pure color. There are several variations, including the kilim slit of flat carpets.

3-19. This example of cramming is extraordinary because it occurs in both warp and weft. The dense crossing requires a satin interlacing. This woven casement of wet-spun gray linen was designed by Alexander Girard.

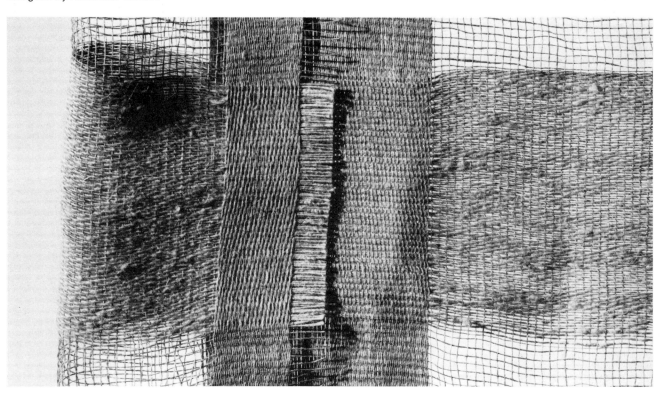

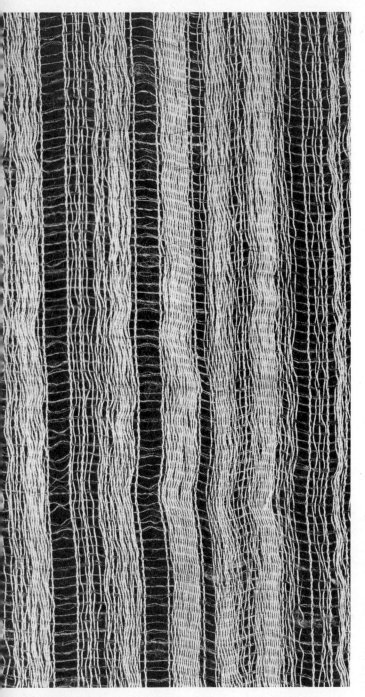

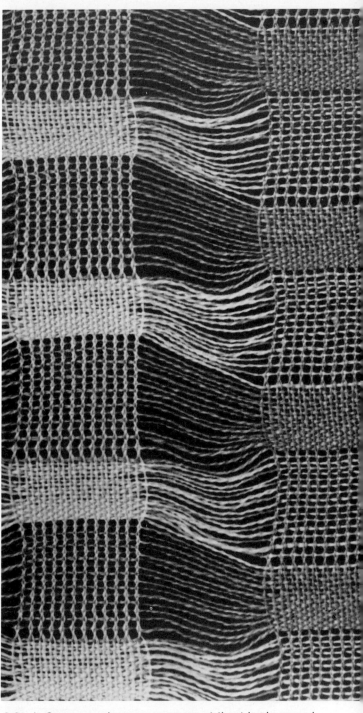

3-20. *Jason*, designed by Win Anderson and Jack Larsen. A warp of fine, plied Egyptian cotton is spaced at various densities. The smooth yarns permit cramming and become wavy when spaced. The voided, or skip-dented, openings are made more secure by the leno-woven warp pairs at their edges.

3-21. In *Gossamer*, a leno-woven casement, the striped warp and weft and the empty, skip-dented bands dramatize the eccentric wefting created with blocks of crammed plain weave.

A number of plain-weave derivatives are based on short *floats* in warp and weft directions—sometimes grouped, sometimes not. While twill and satin weaves may also have systems of warp and weft floats, which are organized in a diagonal or some other orderly alignment, the floats referred to here create linear, rectangular, or open-weave effects, marked by a multiple or mixed order of interlacing with areas of plain weave binding them together. The most important of these are the dimensional huckabacks and piqués, such as the overscaled waffle weave shown in figure 2-8, bedford cords, crepe weaves, and lace weaves—which are not true laces at all.

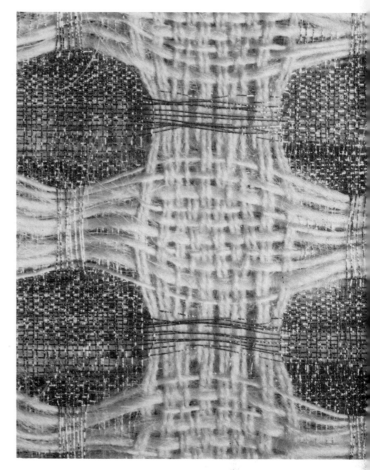

3-22. *Waterford*. An old-fashioned honeycomb weave is transformed into a casement of highly contrasting yarns. The metallic gimp is transparent and light-admitting by day. At night with interior lighting the reflecting metal becomes a wall of light.

3-23. Doubled warp pairs in a leno construction are symmetrically arranged to deflect the heavy weft. The cable-plied linen warp is stable; skip denting and the soft silk weft combine to give superior draping quality. (Photo by Robert L. Beckhard.)

Twill Weave

Twill is the construction of denim and military drill, serge and herringbone, as well as hundreds of other cloths, and is second in importance and universality only to plain weave.

A true twill is constructed by floating one warp and one weft yarn over two or more yarns: the order of interlacing is in a diagonal progression. Unlike the two-harness construction of plain weave, a minimum of three and usually four or more harnesses are required for twill weaves. Twills requiring eight or more harnesses are designated *fancy twills.* Twills may be *balanced,* with an order of interlacing such as over two yarns, under two yarns (2/2). These are identical on both sides. In a three-harness twill the order of interlacing will be under two warp yarns and over one (2/1)—the weave used for denim. This uneven twill will have a warp-faced side and a filling-faced side. Of the simple twill structures, four harnesses are more common than three, and the interlacing order in a warp-faced twill would be designated as 3/1; a weft-faced, 1/3. If, as in denim, the warp and filling colors vary, the color of each side will be different.

Twill constructions allow for a denser, more tightly crammed construction than do equivalent plain weaves, and—for the same stability—they demand it. The longer the float, the denser the construction can be and—to prevent slippage—needs to be.

In addition to the differences noted above, the face and back of unbalanced twills may be used in combination. This is *twill damask,* shown in figure 3-24. If the damask is self-toned, as in table linen, the pattern will derive from highlight and shadow. To gain stronger contrast, different warp and weft colors can be used.

Depending on set, the diagonal progression may be steeper or gentler than the forty-five degrees of a balanced cloth. The direction of the diagonal may be from right to left, from left to right, or a combination of the two, called a *reverse twill* (figure 3-24). Sometimes the diagonal is purposely interrupted or disguised to form a more random mixture, usually with a 1-2-4-3 sequence. This is called a *broken twill.*

If the reversal of direction is in the warp and across the goods, the same construction is called a *herringbone* (see figure 3-25). The combination of reverse twill and herringbone produces a diamond shape, called *bird's-eye,* or *diaper,* pattern (figure 3-25). Figure 3-27 contains all these variations in a long, complex repeat.

3-24. *Round Tower,* woven in Ireland. The polychrome pattern combines reverse twill, damask blocks of a worsted warp and a woolen weft, curves made possible with a jacquard attachment, and striping in both warp and weft. It is also shown in figure C-10.

3-25.

Weft-faced herringbone.

Warp-faced herringbone.

Novelty twill.

Goose-eye, or reverse herringbone.

The basic twill structures alone allow for considerable variation in cloth design, a reason why twills are sometimes characterized as pattern weaves. Derivative weaves are too numerous to categorize and are not so easily grouped under common names. Elaboration of diagonals and diamond configurations abound throughout the history of weaving—especially obvious are colonial and ethnic variations. Perhaps the most distinctive in contemporary fabrics are those related to the twill damasks mentioned above and to the compound cloths that combine twill with other weave structures.

Satin Weave

Satin is the third basic woven construction and the name of cloth woven in this construction. It is basically an extension of a 3/1 twill, in which each warp floats over three wefts and under one. In the simplest *five-point satin* each warp end floats over four wefts and under one. The progression is not diagonal as in twill but staggered to disguise the pattern of weft *tie-downs*. In *seven-* and *eight-point satins* the floats are over six picks and seven picks, respectively. The warps are set closer and the cloth is firmer, often thicker, and more expensive.

A typical satin is woven on a dense warp of fine, smooth filament or combed-and-plied staple yarns. The weave-yarn relationship is more specialized than those of other weaves. The yarns must be packed more tightly in order to create a firm cloth, and, for warp yarns to be set so close together, they must be smooth and strong.

As each of these smooth warp yarns floats over several filling yarns, the cloth surface tends to be very smooth and lustrous, and there is little visual evidence of weft tie-downs. Therefore, characteristics of satin weave are a silky face and a pebbly back. Because of the vertical direction of the cloth, it is stronger and less susceptible to abrasion when draped or upholstered if the warp runs vertically. Satins should not be railroaded.

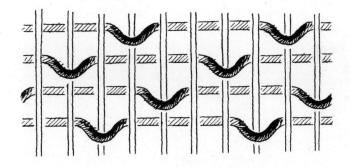

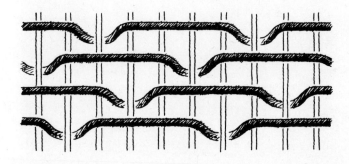

3-26. This diagram shows the construction of warp-faced satin, above, and filling-faced sateen, below. Both are five-point, that is, with a five-end repeat: under four yarns/under one yarn.

Sateen, while employing the same construction as satin, differs in that the floats are found in the horizontal, or filling, direction. Because of this, a wider range of yarns is possible. Typical cloths are sateen drapery linings and antique satin.

A *satin-damask weave* combines areas of satin and sateen construction and, more often than not, is self-toned. In jacquard patterns the basic damask is often combined with brocade and other weaves. Dense stripes of satin weave may also be combined with sheer plain weave (see figure 3-27).

3-27. This damask is composed of a black satin warp and two white sateen wefts. The gray areas are plain-woven. The complex pattern is jacquard-woven of worsted yarns.

C-3. In Jack Larsen's New York apartment this Afghan bedroom doubles as a study for relaxing over afterdinner coffee. In contrast to the cool, light-filled, architectural sparseness of the other rooms, this space is made softly warm and personal by a compilation of fabrics. Paving the ceiling with a mirror doubles the drama. The banquette covers are of hand-printed Thaibok silk, which is outline-quilted. The cushions in silk hand weaves were selected to modulate color, texture, and pattern. A dark, undraped window fabric filters glare and screens the nearby view without "losing" the skylight beyond. The wall fabric is hemp; the carpet, an Afghan-inspired wilton. (Photo courtesy *House Beautiful*, copyright 1974, The Hearst Corporation.)

C-4. Swedish designer Sven Fristedt sits among the patterns he designed as a total environment. Continuity in palette, drawing, and ground cloth permits a profusion of scales and degrees of contrast.

THREE-ELEMENT WEAVES

Three element weaves are constructed with either two warp elements and one weft element or two weft elements woven through a single warp. The third element is so supplemental to the basic weave that it could be picked out to leave a complete simple cloth underneath.

Brocades

The first three-element weave was probably *brocade*, in which the supplemental weft was introduced on the loom as embroidery. Brocading is usually *continuous*, that is, running from selvage to selvage. In continuous brocading long floats may be carried on the underside of an opaque cloth, or they may be clipped off the back of a sheer cloth to create an interplay of densities. In hand weaving this is called *cutwork* (see figure 3-29). Machine clipping is called *broché*. If the surface floats are cut but not clipped away, a fringe, or bangtail, is produced.

An effect similar to broché is produced by printing a plain, patternless brocade cloth. Here, the supplementary yarn, a different fiber than the ground, is dissolved by printing it with acid. The gauze or voile that remains contrasts with the opacity of the unprinted cloth (see figure 4-4).

Both broché and the etched prints described above derive from laid-in, or *discontinuous*, brocades, in which small areas of patterning weft are laboriously woven back and forth in the manner of a tapestry. Not very similar machine versions are *lappet*, *swivel*, and *dotted swiss*.

Warp brocades are similar to weft brocades, except the patterning yarns are vertical. Because they are necessarily continuous, they are simpler and faster to weave. Four-element cloths, which combine warp and weft brocading, are rare.

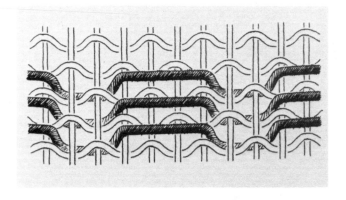

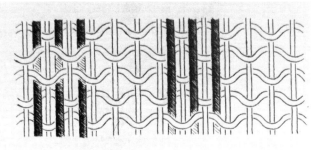

3-28. Brocades in which a supplementary yarn element has been added to plain weave. The top sketch shows a weft brocade; below, a warp brocade in which extra warp yarns form the pattern.

3-29. A jacquard-woven brocade in which the heavy silk underfloats have been cut away to reveal a sheer-cotton leno ground. In India these fabrics are woven and cut by hand and are called cutwork.

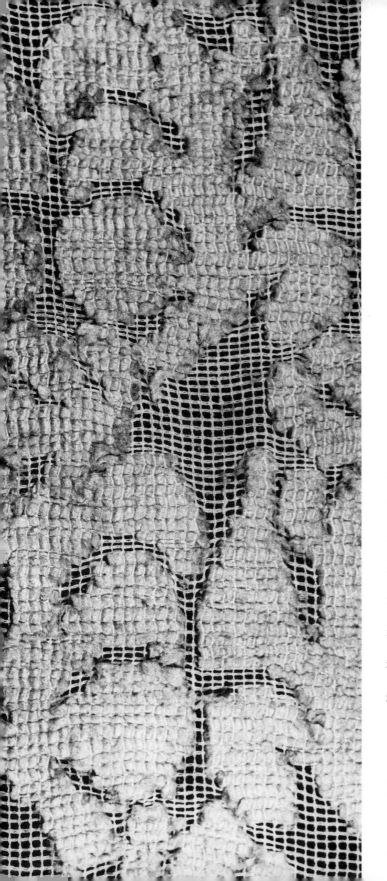

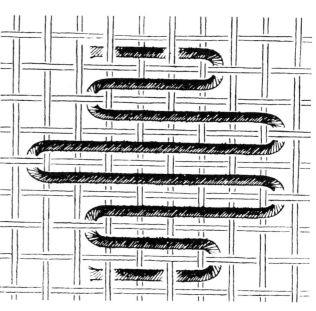

3-30. This diagram illustrates discontinuous brocading, in which the supplementary weft weaves back and forth through the ground. Machine-woven versions are swivel, lappet, and dotted swiss.

Pile Weaves

In addition to a basic ground cloth, *pile weaves* have a supplementary element. Generally, it is an extra set of warp yarns pulled up into the cloth to form a loop on the surface. The simplest of the pile weaves is *terrycloth*, which is formed by releasing a second warp beam to allow a slack in the warp yarns. The slack is then pulled forward into the cloth by the beater to create a series of loops on one or both sides. After weaving and finishing the loops may be sheared for a more velvety surface.

Most pile fabrics and carpets are woven on a *wire loom* with an extra beam, from which the supplementary yarns may be released independently. As illustrated in figure 3-32, these yarns are raised over a flat rod or a round wire. After an inch or more of the cloth is woven, the wires are withdrawn, leaving horizontal rows of uncut loops. *Frieze* and *grospoint* are typical cloths. Friezes may be sheared to resemble cut-pile velvet, but this surface is usually left uncut and appears mossy and mat.

Velvets are woven not with the round wires of frieze but with *cut wires*, which are tipped with a sharp blade. As the wires are withdrawn, these blades cut each loop to create a cut-pile velvet. As in all wire-loom fabrics, including woven-double velvets (see below), the height of the wire determines the height of the pile.

Velvets, which may be of any fiber, have a low (one-eighth inch or less), dense pile. *Velours*, usually linen or cotton, have a somewhat higher pile, often calendered flat in a *panné* finish or crushed. *Plush*, mainly of worsted or mohair yarns, has a still higher pile. Although plush may be crushed or embossed, the pile is usually vertical, bristly, and resistant to both soil and abrasion.

Patterns are created on pile weaves through contrast. In dobby or jacquard patterns and in cloths such as *voided velvets*, areas of pile contrast with a plain ground. *High-and-low* effects are created with two wire heights. *Cut-and-uncut* pile fabrics require both round wires and cut wires.

Unlike velvets, both *velveteen* and *corduroy* have a cut pile composed of *weft* yarns. The pile is created after weaving by cutting weft floats. Both of these fabrics have customarily been made with

cotton. The best qualities use combed, long-staple fiber. Velveteens are mostly used for apparel fabrics.

Thick, large-ribbed, *wide-wale corduroys* are common furniture fabrics. The best grades are serviceable and pleasant enough, but they are almost too common. Fancy corduroys with cables and other allover patterns are less usual. Because corduroys are preshrunk during piece dyeing and launder well, they are good for slipcovers.

Because of their richness and luxury, velvets have always been imitated. Napped and fleeced—even sueded—fabrics are early imitations; knit velours, tufted velours, chenille novelties, and flocked velvets, more recent. Although they are generally intended for mass marketing, some of these cloths are not bad, but they should not be confused with true woven velvets.

The quality and durability of pile fabrics depends on the yarns and fibers used and on the *density* of the pile loops. Density is more costly and more valuable than pile height or thickness of cloth. A thin, long, skimpy pile is not only susceptible to soil and abrasion but is apt to mat down and wither.

Pile loops caught under one shot of weft form a *v-construction*, and pile ends pulled out of the edge of a velvet cutting are in the shape of small vs. If the pile yarn is caught under one weft, raised on the second, then tied down again, the cloth forms a *w-construction*, and the pile ends form small ws.

The advantage of the v-construction is that more pile ends can be packed into the cloth. But if the construction is not firm or if the fibers are silky, pile loss may occur. Losing a few tufts is harmless, but bald patches of exposed ground cloth are uncorrectable. Sound construction and a back coating are the only preventives. A simple test for pile loss is to lightly rub the back of the cloth with a pencil eraser. If the pile quickly pulls out, the fabric is questionable.

Piles may pull out of the face—at least as often as they work out from the underside. This is particularly true if the fabric is riding over a faulty spring or chair frame. The w-construction tends to eliminate these problems, especially if the cloth is woven in such a manner that pile yarns do not even appear on the back of the fabric.

Tenderness or loss of tear strength may rend the ground cloth of pile fabrics. Sometimes this comes from age or exposure. At other times the fault is in the dyeing or finishing. To test the fabric, tear—in *both* directions.

3-31. Pile fabrics such as this frieze are made by raising supplementary warp yarns into a loop pile by means of wires inserted during the weaving process.

3-32. This diagram shows the construction of corduroy. Each supplementary weft yarn that floats over the fine, firmly woven ground is slit to form a vertically ribbed pile.

FOUR-ELEMENT WEAVES

Although double brocades and pile fabrics with two supplementary warps employ four elements, both are rare, and most four-element weaves are *double cloths* of some sort, which have two sets of warp and weft. Most are double plain weaves such as figure 3-33. Because the two cloth layers are usually joined only at the pattern change (otherwise, they lie loosely over one another), they are called *pocket weaves*. Double cloths may, of course, be made with other weaves such as double twill (figure C-5) or combined with brocade or dobby figures.

Matelassé

Matelassé combines areas of single and double cloths within dobby or jacquard patterns. Usually the doubled areas are stuffed with extra yarns to produce a puffy or "quilted" effect. Because it is woven of fine, smooth yarns, matelassé remains a "traditional" fabric, but—at its best—a very beautiful, sensuous one.

Brocatelle

Brocatelle, a richly patterned jacquard weave, usually combines satin and/or twill weaves with plain weave. The high relief is created by stuffing the underside with supplementary yarns, often stiff, wet-spun hemp.

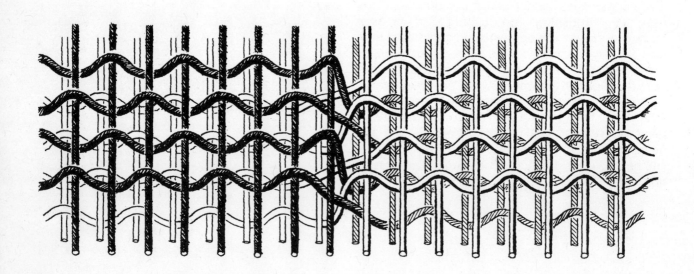

3-33. Double cloth—here, double plain weave—shows the relationship of two layered cloths at the point of intersection. Compare with the photographs of double plain weave (figure C-6) and double twill weave (figures C-5 and 2-5).

MULTIPLE-ELEMENT WEAVES

Woven cloths with five or more elements are not common. The exceptions are velvets and plushes that are *woven double* face-to-face. In this case the two ground cloths are woven one over the other, with the pile yarns weaving up and down between them. While the pile is still on the loom, it is cut through its center, and the two cloths are rolled on separate beams. There is no structural difference between woven-single and woven-double velvets.

Complex, multicolored cut velours and wilton carpets sometimes employ up to four or five supplementary warps. Yarns that do not appear on the face run through the ground, creating a heavier, sturdier, and more expensive fabric.

NEEDLE CONSTRUCTIONS

Besides the woven cloths and the single-element constructions described above, needle-controlled warp knits, laces, and Malimo constructions are used for furnishings—particularly for window fabrics. Because the open-spaced yarns twist and lock in place to permit richly patterned filigrees, these constructions have become increasingly popular. Further innovations may be expected, as well as the invention of other needle-controlled constructions. Tufted and quilted fabrics, also manipulated with needles, are important at present and will be even more so in the future. As they relate to stitchery, we have described them in Part 3, section 6.

3-34. Although this figurative upholstery is called a tapestry, it is not to be confused with plain-woven tapestry joinings. Here, there are six sets of warp yarns, each in a different color. The jacquard attachment selects which warp color will be raised to the surface. (Photo courtesy Stroheim and Romann.)

Knitting

Knitting, which is basically an interlocking series of loops of yarns, may create single-element jerseys and tricots or *double knits* with two or more elements. In jacquard patterns double knits may have a "blistered" relief. They may also be very smooth. Although double knits can just as easily be made stable and unyielding, they do make good stretch-upholstery cloths. That, to date, they are limited by a rather monotonous "apparellike" range of texture is because of the yarns and equipment used—not the process itself.

Rachel Knits

These knits are made on Rachel or similar warp-knitting machines. This flexible, fast-working process is most often based on one set of spaced warp yarns and one or more sets of filling, which stitch back and forth. Within the warps groups of filling "lie" in or between warp groups (see figure 3-35). Although Rachel machines mainly produce lacy casements, rigid and stretch upholsteries are also in production—as are carpets.

Laces

A wide range of openwork lacy cloths is produced by the broadest variety of hand and machine techniques. Furnishings laces may be single-element *bobbin laces* such as figure 3-37, but most are *nottingham laces* with warp and filling elements. This construction is fast, flexible, very wide, and potentially extraordinary in the broad range of jacquard-controlled filigree patterns. The weakness of these laces lies in the fact that they shrink during cleaning, especially the heavy, handsome cotton ones, which shrink five to ten percent. Since lace stretchers are no longer common, the safest course is to launder the fabric prior to makeup. Once they are preshrunk, these cloths machine-wash very well. Heat-set polyester nottinghams tend to be stable and shrink-resistant—but dull.

3-35. This Rachel warp-knit casement has warp groups of fine yarns and heavy wefts that knit up one warp group, then skip to the next. This construction is slip-resistant and snagproof.

3-36. *Interplay*, the original warp-knit casement, employs diagonals for stability. The saran slit-film yarn is not only fire-retardant and soil-resisting but dimensionally stable when heat-set. An installation is shown in figure 2-2.

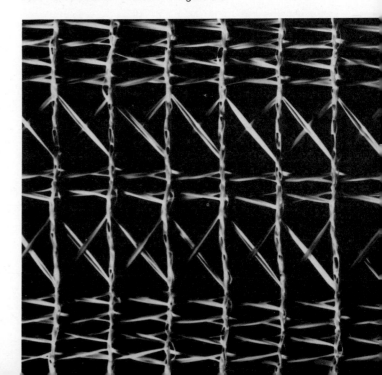

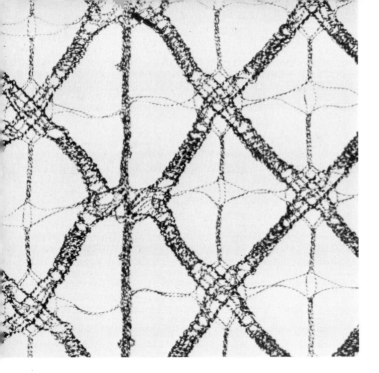

Malimo

An East German invention, *Malimo* is one of the newest fabric constructions and surely the fastest means of interlacing yarns. Instead of carrying wefts across the loom one at a time, Malimo, in one fell swoop, lays wide banks of weft—twelve inches or more—across a warp of fine filaments. Then hundreds of monofilament stitching yarns (a third element) furiously knit the weft onto the warp (see figure 3-39). These stitching yarns are often simple chain stitching, which is susceptible to unchaining, like any flour sack, if the open end of the chain is accessible. In casements or draperies the open end should be at the top. Other, less common Malimo constructions simulate terry and other woven cloths.

3-37. *Baghdad* is an authentic bobbin lace, a single-element hand technique on ancient equipment in which narrow strips are joined together. (The joining is the heavy vertical on the left.) In addition to their great freedom of form, such laces are slip-resistant.

3-38. Although it is called bobbin cloth, this is a nottingham lace designed as a patchwork of several filigrees. The vertical bands ensure stability. These cloths are usually very wide.

3-39. Malimo is a speedy new fabric technique. The closeup of a Malimo casement with an etching print shows the netlike construction.

5. Finishing

Finishing is one of the broadest and most general of all fabric terms. It includes hundreds of postproduction processes and treatments to make cloth more suitable for a specific end use. Some finishes are physical, some chemical; some supply additives. Some are very temporary, others durable, and many completely permanent. Finishes can make fabric softer, stiffer, or resistant to certain kinds of abuse. Sometimes one finish, such as permanent press, makes a fabric more susceptible to another problem, such as poor soil release. Generally speaking, these special finishes are deceiving only to the extent that they distract attention from cloth quality per se. Still, all are useful for certain purposes, and cloth finishing has become one of the liveliest aspects of fabric technology.

Most cloths undergo several finishing processes, and yet we speak in terms of *a* finish. The discrepancy lies in a tendency to ignore the standard finishing processes accomplished early on in order to focus on a single one that gives a special appearance, such as glazing, or a special property, such as flame retardance. Different finishes may be applied at different stages of postproduction processing. Scouring, for instance, is first; a soil-retardant finish is usually last, following the standard finishes and dyeing, printing, and other conversion steps.

STANDARD FINISHES

Generally speaking, fabric as it comes from the loom or knitting machine is about as ready for consumption as an unbaked cake. The least ready are soft, dense cloths such as blanketing, terry, and outing flannel, which come off the loom looking—and feeling—like sheer, stiff mosquito netting. Depending on the fiber used, unfinished fabrics are full of either natural grease, gum, or sizing added to the yarns during production. These substances and other impurities are released by the process of *scouring*, or *boiling off*. The cloth is simultaneously shrunk to a density controlled by a tenter frame, and the fibers within the yarn bulk, or *bloom*, to make a fuller, softer cloth.

At this stage goods are usually bleached, dyed, and/or prepared for printing. Bleaches may be single or double; certain cloths are also dyed white, i.e., treated with optical brighteners to reflect ultraviolet light. Cottons and linens are often *mercerized* (see Part 3, section 2) and preshrunk. Thermoplastic man-made fibers are *heat-set* to make them permanently conform to their interlacing pattern. Wools may be *carbonized* in acid to remove vegetable matter, then *sheared* or *singed* to remove surface fibers. Tweeds are pressed with a fabric-covered roller. Worsteds and cloths of most other fibers are *calendered*, or pressed under steel rollers to produce some degree of luster. Similarly, linens undergo *beetling*, a pounding action that flattens the yarns to a ribbon-like profile.

Another approach to finishing is often taken by small producers of luxury furnishings fabrics, especially those who work with a variety of yarns and fibers. Instead of elaborate finishing, which requires complex equipment and more production time, these mills begin with *clean* yarns—yarns that are prescoured, bleached, and often yarn-dyed. After mending and sponging, these *loom-state* goods are ready for sale. The clarity and texture of the yarns is at a maximum. Any tendency to slip or ravel is often corrected by a backing (see Part 3, section 6). If these fabrics are to be used at the window, they are usually *decatized*, that is, cold-water shrunk, which improves hand and draping quality, reduces raveling, and usually preshrinks the goods sufficiently for dry cleaning but not laundering (see Part 2, section 1).

SPECIAL FINISHES

The character of some fabrics is completely determined by a special finish.

Ciré (from the French, meaning wax) is a high-luster glaze produced with wax or resins and hot rollers on silk, cotton, or synthetics—originally to imitate Chinese lacquered silks. Durability varies. The *wet look* is a recent version.

Embossing is the process of pressing a relief pattern into the cloth surface with a hot, engraved roller. If the cloth passes between a positive and a negative roller, the relief is proportionately stronger. Any fabric may be used, but pile fabrics, coated fabrics, and papers are the most successful. Cloths woven of thermoplastic fibers, including wool and mohair plushes, emboss more or less permanently.

Fulling, particular to wools, is shrinking, controlled to various degrees. It may be carried far enough to produce a felted fabric, e.g., a melton. More often—as in flannels, wool broadcloths, and the various fleeces—fulling is combined with napping, shearing, and calendering and is carried only to the point of closing up the weave to give it the proper density.

Glazing is a general term for polishing smooth cloths with waxes or resins and hot steel rollers. It produces a duller, less waxy finish than ciré. Polished cottons and *chintz* are typical glazed cottons. The permanence of the glaze varies considerably: the Everglaze process is relatively durable.

Moiré, which produces a characteristic swirling, grained pattern with reflective highlights, is accomplished by feeding two ribbed fabrics (such as faille) face to face between two smooth rollers. High pressure on the rollers causes the ribs of each fabric to partially deflect and flatten those of the other. With thermoplastic cloths such as silk, acetate, and synthetics the effect is permanent. Moiré is also imitated with engraved cylinders, but the result is less miraculous, and there is necessarily a pattern repeat.

Napping is raising fiber ends to the surface by means of rollers covered with emery cloth, metal teeth, or teasels. If they are sheared, fibers on the downy surface may resemble a pile. Weaves or knits of any fiber may be napped or brushed for better warmth or hand. Typical napped cloths are cotton or nylon suedecloth, blanketings, fleeces, wool broadcloths, and flannels.

FUNCTIONAL FINISHES

The term *functional finish* does not imply that standard and special finishes are *not* functional: it is an attempt to classify treatments that are less concerned with hand and appearance than with *performance*. Most of them involve immersion, so they are also called *chemical finishes* or *wet finishes*.

Mothproof finishes protect protein fibers and fiber blends from attack by moths and carpet beetles. Normally, the chemical agent is added to the dyebath. However, fabrics that have not been mothproofed, such as exotic imports, can also be treated in a finished-cloth state. Most wools—and all that have a Wool Mark label—come with a mothproof finish. If a fabric is not so labeled, make an inquiry. If necessary, goods can be treated by a custom finisher.

Wrinkle resistance is not provided by a finish but by a series of processes to deter crushing and wrinkles. Some fabrics—most wools and mohairs, for example—have this quality inherently. Others, such as thermoplastic fibers, are given a *permanent press*—a "memory" for flatness imparted during heat setting. Blends of thermoplastics and cellulosics may have resins added to ensure a permanent press. Cellulosic fibers, especially cottons and rayons, are often resin-treated for crease resistance. The best-known treatment for linen is Tebilizing; unfortunately, it is not common in furnishings.

There are two commonsense cures for fabric wrinkles. Newly hung draperies should be lightly sprayed with a fine mist of clean water. This tends to soften and weight the fabric sufficiently to release wrinkles gathered in transit and installation. Thin fabric slipcovers and bedspreads can be treated with silicone or some other soil-resistant finish. These same resins give body and reduce hydrophilic properties.

Antiseptic or *antibacterial finishes* are useful in preventing the growth of mildew and other microorganisms. They are particularly recommended and may be required for institutions or tropical climates. They may be temporary or durable and can be applied by the producer or custom finisher.

Soil-repellent finishes are useful in many instances, particularly for upholsteries and some wall fabrics. Many fabrics today come with a soil-repellent finish, and custom finishers stand ready to supply one. The biggest danger is in expecting too much from such a finish. Cloths that are normally susceptible to soil and light colors that show soil easily may be improved by such a finish, but they are *not* soilproof, nor are they apt to be as resistant as, for instance, a soundly constructed wool. *Silicone finishes* tend to repel water and thus to resist spills of water-based liquids and soiling. *Scotchgard* and *Zepel* (trade names of soil-repellent fluorochemical finishes) resist both oil- and water-borne stains. They also make for better soil release, especially if spills are blotted and sponged immediately. *Soil-release finishes* are important only for furnishings fabrics and table linens that have been treated for permanent press with a high-polyester-content and/or resin finish. Without a soil-release finish, oily substances in particular are impossible to remove if they are not treated immediately. *Antistatic finishes*, although often temporary, are useful in reducing static electricity in certain synthetics, particularly nylons. They increase moisture content and thus diminish the static electricity that attracts and holds soil. Newer nylons developed for special uses, such as carpets, have a built-in antistatic property.

Flame-retardant finishes have come a long way since their introduction in the 1940s. Their old tendencies toward discoloration, tenderness, and hyperabsorbency (which causes dripping) are long gone. If there is any doubt about the effects of treatment, a trial sample should be sent to the custom finisher. At this writing acrylics still cannot be treated. Progress is being made toward built-in flame retardance, but it is not yet ready for production. Some sheer polyesters or polyester blends present problems of performance, appearance, and finish. Most other cloths can be treated satisfactorily and durably (see Part 2, section 1).

Both fire codes and developments in fire retardancy change so frequently—and, in the case of codes, so locally—that current information must be constantly sought. The most authoritative source of information is the National Fire Protection Association (NFPA), 470 Atlantic Avenue, Boston, Massachusetts 02210. The NFPA can supply up-to-date codes and rulings on textile materials used in public buildings. The offices of local fire marshals will answer inquiries about city codes—or the lack of them. Government buildings may have more stringent regulations than public buildings. More and more states are joining the ranks of those that already have legislation covering fire safety. Expect more action in the future from the Product Safety Commission, working with other federal agencies and trade associations such as the National Furniture Association. Legislation on carpeting and mattress assemblies is well established (though test procedures are not). As for draperies, some city codes recommend acceptable fire-retardant finishes or require conformity with specified test procedures. Codes for upholstery fabrics, undercushioning, and plastics in furnishing products are yet to be defined, but many research laboratories are actively working on these potential fire hazards.

6. Compound Cloths

In addition to all the fabric constructions described in Part 3 and the special cloths created by finishing and other conversion techniques, there is still another category of major and growing importance. This includes cloths, such as embroidered and tufted fabrics, that are *compounded* by another yarn element or—by one means or another—*layered* in two or more thicknesses. All are, in a sense, *converted* (see Part 5, section 3). However, in many cases the added element is so much more involved or costly than the base cloth that allusion to conversion becomes inappropriate.

EMBROIDERIES

Embellishing a fabric with yarn, feathers, quills, bangles, or sequins is in many cultures older than cloth making itself. Consider, for instance, American Indian beadwork and quillwork on buckskin. As the most popular of handcrafts, embroidery is a universal language binding East and West, past and present. Most hand embroidery on the market today is imported, and much of that is "antique." Dominant in furnishings are Kashmir *crewel embroideries*, in which wool yarns are chain-stitched onto homespun cotton. The paisleylike motifs are as traditional as the technique. An exception is the contemporary version shown in figure 3-40.

3-40. This modern crewel pattern retains the traditional wool yarn, which is chain-stitched to a cotton ground. Because every stitch is made by hand, colors may number in the dozens. (Photo courtesy Stroheim and Romann.)

Most domestic embroidery today is machine embroidery. Because it is made on a schiffli machine, it is called *schiffli embroidery*. It is most often sparse, with relatively few stitches and broad, open areas of unstitched ground. Fine and sheer, schiffli cloth is intended for bedroom curtaining or as trimming for linens. The thinness is not accidental: costs are based on the number of stitches and the amount of yarn used. Characteristic of schiffli embroidery is its technique, in which the decorative yarn does not penetrate the cloth: it is held in place by a binding thread stitched through from the back. Schiffli is also the only fabric that is worked *sideways*. Usually in ten-yard lengths, the cloth is fed selvage first into the huge machine in rows parallel to the length of the goods. Thousands of needles stitch simultaneously. For this reason embroideries—both schifflis and crewels—are sold in short pieces.

Variations on schiffli include an appliqué in which two cloths are embroidered together, then part of the top layer is cut away; and schiffli lace, achieved by embroidering a grill-like pattern with very compact stitches, then burning away the ground cloth with acid so that only the "lace" remains.

TUFTED FABRICS

Tufted fabrics are embroideries in the sense that yarn is *needled* through a finished cloth. They are characteristically pile fabrics, produced at very high speeds and often in widths up to eighteen feet. The pile may be all cut, all loop, or a combination of the two. A hand-guided, single-needle machine, or *electric pistol*, is capable of producing freely drawn multicolor patterns with considerable speed. Multi-needle tufting, in which the whole width is tufted simultaneously, is extraordinarily fast—so much so that an increasing number of upholstery "velours" are produced by tufting. "Chenille" bedspreads are also tufted, and today almost all rugs and carpets are tufted. To secure the tufts, the back is usually coated with a rather heavy latex.

3-41. *Magnum* is a schiffli embroidery in which most of the mirrored Mylar ground is covered with thousands of stitches in eight different colors. It is very heavy, production is slow, and costs are high.

QUILTING

Quilting—stitching together two or more layers of fabric—is a very old technique. Depending on the thickness of the fiber layer between the face and the backing cloth, quilting provides various degrees of softness, relief, and warmth. It also cushions abrasion. Traditionally, the center of the sandwich was one or more layers of cotton batting. Today, the batting is often made of polyester or acrylic fibers or of synthetic foam.

Traditionally, *hand quilting* was often combined with appliqué and patchwork. Today, quilting is more often an accessory to a printed cloth. The stitches are machine-made by any of several methods. The most versatile and by far the most costly is *hand-guided* quilting, done with a single-needle machine much like an oversized Singer. The three most popular types are *outline quilting*, in which the stitch follows the motif of a printed fabric; *vermicelli*, which is an allover, noodlelike squiggle; and *trapunto*, in which only portions of the cloth are quilted and stuffed, often in a centered medallion. The top stitch may be simple and nearly invisible or a cordlike chain stitch. Because of its cost and flexibility, most hand-guided quilting is done on a custom basis. As in quilted arms and cushions for a plain chair or sofa, simple fabrics are often combined with quilting to good effect and at considerable savings.

In *machine quilting* a whole width of cloth is passed through a multiple-needle machine. A variety of simple geometric patterns are available at a cost of about thirty percent of hand-guided quilting. Even faster and cheaper than this is a whole new range of quilting techniques that employ adhesive or fusion instead of stitches with thread. As fast as printing and sometimes even less expensive, these methods are popular on the retail and ready-made markets, but should be checked for permanence in dry cleaning or laundering—whichever is appropriate. ·

BONDED FABRICS

In the apparel field two fabrics are often bonded together, the top one for its surface quality, the bottom one for strength and support. This is less common in furnishings. Liquid or spray backings are used more frequently. The exception is wall fabric bonded to paper (see Part 2, section 3). *Laminated fabrics* are also created by adhering fabric layers, but the *substrate*, or underlayer, is of synthetic foam. Sometimes the foam is the center of a three-layered sandwich. Chief uses are in stretch-knit upholsteries and in wall fabrics.

Warp laminates, a set of parallel and vertical yarns bonded to paper, are becoming increasingly important as wall coverings (see figure 2-9). Thickness and density, quantity and quality of yarns range from commercial to luxurious. Tear strength and resistance to delamination or peeling are usually adequate. The heavy wool versions offer soil resistance.

BACKED FABRICS

Backing is the correct term for liquid or spray coatings applied to the back of fabrics (see Part 2, sections 2 and 3). Backings provide stability, resistance to slippage and fraying, and increased durability. The lightest of backings, called *kiss coats*, are hardly evident and are drapable. Heavier backings may be too stiff for a lightweight fabric.

COATED FABRICS

Coated fabrics are top-coated over a knit, woven, or nonwoven base. The best known are vinyl upholsteries such as Naugahyde. Some of the thinner glove-leather types employ polyester or polyurethane for the coating. Durability and resistance to abrasion tend to be excellent, and cracking and delamination are no longer a problem, but even the breathable types tend to be too dense for comfort (see Part 2, section 2).

PART 4: COLORING

Of all the aspects of fabric, coloring is the most difficult to fit into a description of the production continuum. In the preparation of a fabric color may come *first*, as in solution-dyed fibers, or *last*, as in pad dyeing, in which color is rolled on just before the goods are packed for marketing. Interestingly enough, both extremes derive from an economic premise—the first, to eliminate coloring as a separate process; the second, to keep inventories undifferentiated for as long as possible.

Although *coloring* is not a trade term nor one with wide usage, it is useful in describing the wide assortment of means by which fabrics get color. Today, the universal terms *dyeing* and *printing* are not broad enough to include all methods of building color into cloth.

Although *conversion* (see Part 5, section 3) is an inclusive term covering piece dyeing, printing, and other processes, it does not include color obtained before or during fabric production.

From points of view as divergent as aesthetics and economics, designing and production, sales and selection, fabric color—its character, quality, timeliness, and durability—is at least as important and problematic as any other aspect of fabric. Color is beauty, fashion, the key to class sales and even more to mass ones. Color is profit and loss, the darling of the industry, and an absolute nightmare.

4-1. *Conquistador*, an authentic wax batik, has sufficient natural variation to create a lively nuance of color tonalities. The velvet ground is first blocked with a hot wax, then cooled, cracked, and dyed. After the wax is removed, the cloth is dyed again and refinished.

1. Dyes and Dyeing

Perhaps the biggest distinction in coloring processes is between goods produced in color and goods colored in a conversion or postproduction phase. Piece dyeing is the principal conversion technique, but printing and other processes are also important. What follows here is a description of coloring within the production process.

UNDYED AND NATURAL COLORS

Most cloth is produced with undyed yarns and bleached, dyed, or otherwise converted afterward. While there has been in recent years a growing movement away from the white shirt, sheet, and towel, furnishings fabrics have exhibited a countermovement toward using fabric in an undyed and unprinted state. This is due partly to less big-city appetite for clean, light-reflecting whites and partly to economic considerations. Adding color to fabric can increase the selling price from ten to more than a hundred percent.

While undyed fabrics have an increasing appeal, natural fibers in natural colors are booming. With as little bleaching and finishing as possible, their naturalness is at a peak. Canvaslike cottons are favored, as are gray and boiled linens, while silks, wools, and alpacas with admixtures of natural beige, gray, or brown seem special indeed.

Although natural colors do not fade, it should be pointed out that they will change. Cellulosics bleach in sunlight and lighten when laundered. Protein fibers yellow and darken. Grasses and hard fibers alter the most: bleached sisal, jute, and coir tend to return to their dark natural states. But in most cases this changing, aging, and mellowing is acceptable: it is not a loss of beauty.

SOLUTION DYEING

In *solution dyeing* (or *dope dyeing*) the coloring agent is added to the liquid solution before it is extruded through the spinneret into man-made fiber. Because the color is inherent to the fiber, this is the most permanent form of coloring. Yarns made from such fiber will also be completely uniform in color. If production is high enough, this is also an economical method of dyeing. The limitations are: (1) solution dyeing is limited to man-made fibers; (2) economic runs must be so large that color ranges are necessarily limited and planned long in advance. Determining color before the yarn is even spun requires advance commitment, larger inventories, and extra risk. Also, working with colored fiber tends to contaminate spinning equipment. Although blending solution-dyed fibers into heather mixtures makes for a more interesting yarn in a broader color range, it is rarely used.

STOCK DYEING

Dyeing fiber staple or *stock* before it is spun is the natural-fiber equivalent to solution dyeing. The advantages are complete penetration, a tendency to colorfastness, and very *level*, even, nonstreaky dye lots. Because stock dyeing is expensive and requires a long lead time, its use is limited to woolen fibers in heather-spun yarns.

YARN DYEING

Most colored yarns are dyed in yarn rather than fiber form. How they are dyed varies with the size and type of production. *Beaker* (literally "in the cup") dyeing is used in the color laboratory to determine the dye formula. *Skein*, or *hank*, dyeing, i.e., dyeing loose skeins of yarns in a large vat in which the skeins, liquid, or both are kept in motion, is still used by small and custom producers. It is the standard handcraft method. As lots may be small, it is the most flexible. But since both dyeing and winding costs are the highest, skein dyeing is used less and less.

PACKAGE DYEING

The *package* used in this process is a small, perforated tube. Usually three hundred to one thousand one-pound packages are stacked into a special dye kettle in such a manner that first the dye liquid, then the rinse bath can be forced through the yarn. Whole warps wound onto perforated beams are often dyed in the same manner, resulting in even larger economies. On a less industrial level, warps are sometimes dyed in a rope form, much like a very long skein.

PIECE DYEING

Dyeing *in the piece*, after construction and scouring, is the most popular way of coloring fabric. It becomes more so each year, for not only is piece dyeing the most efficient and least costly, but it comes nearest to the end of the production cycle and closest to the point of sale. In other words, piece dyeing has all the advantages of a conversion process.

There are some limitations. Dense constructions such as canvas or hard, tightly twisted yarns may have poor dye penetration. Particularly if the end use entails considerable abrasion—as in upholstery—the undyed fiber or yarn will become apparent at the point of crossing. Fabrics that are thin or openly constructed, fabrics with lofty yarns or of hydrophilic fibers such as wool and rayon, and cut-pile fabrics tend not to have penetration problems. The test for dye penetration can be as simple as examining the unraveled fabric and its twisted yarns.

C-5. The fabric on the walls and ceilings is a nylon stretch knit, which is applied to wooden ribs with blind-tacked seams (see Part 2, section 3). A characteristic of freely stretched fabric is that all curves are "perfect." The same fabric, printed and laminated to foam, is upholstered on the settee. The chairs are covered in a plain-woven stretch worsted. (Photo by Grigsby courtesy *House & Garden*, copyright 1968, Conde Nast Publications, Inc.)

C-6. *Jezebel*, hand-screened on cotton velvet without overlays but with a crisp outline in the manner of Chinese cloisonné. Some of its thirteen colors are close in hue and value; others are sharply contrasting.

C-7. *Primavera*, hand-screened on cotton velvet, achieves a special quality from the knowing use of color printed over color to build a rich surface. Drawing by Don Wight.

C-8. *Chan-Chan*, a fold-dyed fabric, epitomizes the sensuous expression of liquid dyes seeping through thirsty fibers. Dyed in Kenya by the late Eliza Wilcox.

C-6.

C-7.

C-8.

Piece-dyed fabrics occasionally shade from selvage to center or from one end of the piece to the other. This can be checked by examination and is no more serious than similar problems with yarn dyes. There is, however, a certain "Russian-roulette" kind of risk in piece dyeing. Cloths that seem homogeneously white on entering the dye bath sometimes emerge with streaks or bars caused by mixed lots of yarn or flecks of contaminating lint or other impurities. Exotic hand-wovens are particularly risky. But the loss is usually the producer's—not the consumer's.

Piece dyeing has a somewhat deserved reputation for fugitive color. The fault is not with piece dyeing per se but with dyeing in small lots, often on a custom basis, without trials and testing. This is usually done by *beck dyeing*, which is suitable to a short production run. In beck dyeing fabric moves through the dye box in a relaxed, ropelike form. Texture and fullness are retained.

Jig dyeing and *pad dyeing* are very inexpensive, efficient, and widely used, particularly for lightweight fabrics. Because the fabric is dyed full-width, the texture and fullness of hand may be pulled out under tension or flattened by rollers—faults that do not affect many fabrics. In any case the loss is immediate and visible: there are no further or later ill effects. The pad-dyeing process may also be used to apply special finishes or—as on fiberglass—pigmented color.

Overdyeing, a type of piece dyeing, is occasionally done on a cloth that already contains some dyed yarns or fibers. Most often, the dyed fiber is black, usually stock-dyed. It will remain black, showing a pattern through the piece-dyed color. Black-and-white heathers are sometimes overdyed in the same way. Because this double dyeing is expensive, it is often replaced by cross dyeing (described below).

COMBINATION DYEING

Union dyeing is employed to obtain solid color in a cloth made up of fibers with different dye affinities. Wool-and-cotton or linen-and-polyester blends, for instance, require matching two classes of dyestuffs. Cotton-and-rayon (both cellulosic)

or wool-and-mohair (both protein) blends do not. Especially in cloths that combine yarns with different dye affinities, *cross dyeing* may be used to good purpose. Color effects such as the checks and plaids normally found only in yarn-dyed goods can be achieved with cross dyeing. A yarn such as acetate can be left white or dyed a different color than the cotton it was woven with. Cross dyeing in three colors is more difficult but quite possible. To immerse a solid white cloth and pull out a brilliant plaid is like writing with invisible ink but better!

With yarns of intimately blended fibers heathered and frosted effects are possible. *Modified dye affinity* is a more recent development. By combining normal and modified yarns, cross-dyed effects are possible within a single generic fiber. Du Pont pioneered fiber modification with its *cationic-dyeing* process, in which an all-nylon fabric could be cross-dyed with two or three dyestuffs. A simpler modification is the *deep-dye* fiber, which, when dyed with normal yarns of the same family, produces a darker, tone-on-tone effect.

CLASSES OF DYES

A *dye* or *dyestuff* is a soluble coloring matter that in certain conditions will actually fuse with a fiber molecule. Dyestuffs are almost always dispersed in water to form a dyebath or dye liquor. Fiber, yarn, or cloth is immersed in the dyebath, usually heated to a carefully regulated temperature. When the fiber has reached the desired shade, it is rinsed and dried. With certain dyes *mordants* or *aftertreatments* are necessary for brilliance or permanence. Mordants are chemicals that combine with dyes in the cloth: they may be applied before or after a fiber, yarn, or cloth is dyed. Aftertreatments, often chemical and physical, are applied to dyed and finished cloth.

A fiber is a chemical substance; so is a dyestuff. When a dyestuff will combine with a fiber, we say that it has an *affinity* for that fiber, and specific dyes are used for the various classifications of fibers. For convenience the thousands of dyestuffs are divided into *classes of dyes*. Dyestuffs within a class have the same dye affinity, require similar temperatures, and produce similar—but not the same—fastness.

The classes of dyes include the following. *Acid dyes* or *premetallized acids* are used primarily for protein, acrylic, and nylon fibers. *Basic*, or *cationic*, *dyes* are used for acrylics, modacrylics, and specially treated polyesters and nylons. *Direct* and *developed direct dyes* are used for cellulosics. *Disperse dyes* are used for acetates, polyesters, nylons, and acrylics; a combination of high pressure and high temperature is often necessary to fix the dye, and acetates have a tendency toward gas fading (see below). *Fiber-reactive*, or *procion*, *dyes* are used for cellulosics and sometimes for wools and silks. They produce bright shades with excellent fastness and are more washable, but the authors do not favor them. *Naphthol dyes* produce the most brilliant reds in cellulosics. *Sulfur dyes* produce heavy shades of black and brown in cellulosics. *Vat dyes* are also used for cellulosics; they tend to be brilliant and fast.

Both vat dyes and developed dyes *develop*. Unlike photographic film, they do not evolve from nothing to a color but from dull to bright—a dull bronze to a clear red, for instance. Developed dyes tend to resist fading.

PIGMENTS

Pigments are not dyes: they do not combine with fiber molecules but are physically bound to a cloth by means of resin binders. Pigments are printed on cloth or applied by pad-dyeing methods. They are the only means of coloring such hydrophobic fibers as asbestos and fiberglass. Because they are mat, they contrast favorably with a lustrous cloth. White and very dark pigments tend to be thick and opaque. Their opacity provides a special dimension if they are printed on sheers. Unfortunately, the whites tend to yellow, and the thick pigments are especially vulnerable to crocking and abrasion.

The advantages of pigments are: (1) they tend to be inexpensive; (2) they can be applied to all fibers; (3) they are easy to match; and (4) they do not fade in light (but often do in the wash). For these reasons they are often used by custom printers and students. On the negative side, pigments have the look of being *on*, not *in* the fabric. They lack the transparency of dyes, they are sensitive to abrasion, and they may feel stiff or sticky. Some pigments, such as those printed on sheets and towels, are thinned down to an inklike consistency, and penetration and luminosity are better. Metallized fabrics and printed metallics are necessarily pigments. Their quality and resistance depend on the binders used.

NATURAL AND MANUFACTURED DYES

Most dyestuffs used to be *natural*—usually vegetable, occasionally animal or mineral in origin. Today, almost all dyestuffs are *manufactured*. The tradition of dyeing is rich, however, and there are romantic myths about ancient methods.

A vegetable dye does not produce more beautiful or more enduring colors than dyes in use today. The legend of durability comes primarily from ancient cloths or carpets that have never seen the light of day. The "beauty" is usually a combination of the enriching variation within a hand-spun yarn and a lively, somewhat streaky dye job—plus a color tradition developed over centuries and the concentration and care of an artisan working on one piece at a time. Yes, it is beautiful.

The impact of manufactured dyes on craft traditions has been earth-shaking and in most cases disastrous. Too often, they were used full-strength and unmixed, and mordants and rinses were omitted. The too raw, too garish colors soon faded or—worse—bled onto adjacent white grounds. The conversion from local hand spinning to sleazy, mill-spun yarns came at the same time and aggravated the tragedy.

On the bright side, we now have an almost total palette of color to choose from. So do the artisans of the third world—their palette includes the extraordinary Siamese and Peruvian pinks, which were not available in vegetable colors. It is also to the credit of the great international dye houses that they now have competent technicians working with remote craftsmen to develop a workable dye technology.

DYE COSTS

The cost of dyeing is an important factor, not so much in terms of performance as of color quality. Color costs money. Coloring may range from five percent to fifty percent of the selling price. To begin with, there are considerable cost differences among various classes of dyes, and even within one class one colorant may be costlier than another. Depth of shade is an even larger factor—a deep navy needs twenty times more dyestuff than a pastel blue. Fully saturated, brilliant colors generally cost the most. The size of the run is perhaps the largest factor. Dyeing in small lots is expensive; so is customizing color. Mixing colored yarns with natural ones may save money; printing with more than full coverage (all of the cloth plus some areas twice) costs a premium; and so on.

KEY TERMS

Bars, *color bars*, *bar marks*, and *barrés*, all of which mean the same thing, are horizontal bands extending from selvage to selvage. They may be caused by changes within the filling or by a tension differential.

Bleeding is not fading but the running of one color into another. It usually occurs during washing, and sometimes in production or finishing.

Colorfastness is resistance to fading from light, cleaning, perspiration, abrasion, or gas fumes. Because no single dyestuff is proof against all contingencies, specific dyes are selected for specific end uses (see above).

Dry crocking is the rubbing off of excess colorants. The danger is not in a loss of inherent color but in contamination of other fabrics such as clothing (see Part 2, section 2). *Wet crocking* occurs when the cloth is moist.

Gas fading usually means a change—not a loss—of color. It is caused by airborne impurities such as carbon monoxide and nitrogenous oxides. Untreated acetates are particularly subject to gas fading.

Match is a relative term that refers to the "same" color from one dye lot to another. Dyers insist on an allowance for "commercial tolerance." Sometimes this allowance is more than the purchasers care to tolerate. It is useful to consider the production lot not in terms of match to standard but in relation to other colors in the room. Sometimes these can be modified more easily than the specific fabric in question.

Metamerism, in relation to color match, refers to colors that match under one light source but not another. The wide use of fluorescent and neon lights has increased instances of metamerism.

Shade loosely means "color," especially in relation to match. Fabrics may be *off-shade*, not off-color.

Shading is the fault of color gradation from selvage to center or from end to end.

A *standard* or *master* is an approved production sample and dye formula. Each succeeding dye lot will vary somewhat: some may be more beautiful than others.

2. Printing

Fabric printing is in a dynamic phase with an accelerated momentum toward innovation and, at the same time, speed and efficiency. And although printing is not the only star in the future of fabric, it will surely be found in more guises and in broadening arrays of techniques and end uses.

Aside from technological and economic breakthroughs, printed fabric—more than most consumer goods—is capable of exploiting our vast legacies of fabric tradition and applied ornament in general. Although there are more bad prints than great ones and too many that are trite and boring, particularly in furnishings, printed cloth can and does reinterpret our enriching traditions with more conviction and more verve than reproduction furniture or "traditional" table appointments.

At the same time, printed fabrics have taken bold strides in a contemporary direction. Good, original designs do turn up in printed fabric, usually without design credit and usually in apparel or in imports. The point is not that we need pattern everywhere, but that printing—as an important, visible aspect of fabric conversion—is in tune with our time.

KEY TERMS

A *strike-off* is a color trial on cloth of one or more pattern repeats. It is mostly used to establish color lines, to check pattern, and to prove cloth and finish.

A *blotch*, as in *blotch printing*, is a printed solid-color background that blots out all areas of the ground-cloth color left between the pattern forms. A large printed area may present problems of penetration and absorption. A fitted cloth is *overengraved*, or *overprints*, the pattern a thirty-second to a quarter of an inch.

Coverage refers to the percentage of cloth that is printed. In a linear-printed casement coverage may be as little as ten percent. In an elaborate, overprinted fabric such as the one shown in figure C-16 coverage may approach one hundred forty percent. The amount of coverage usually affects printing costs.

Dye affinity is the tendency of a specific fiber to absorb various dyestuffs (see Part 4, section 1).

Halftones are subtle shadings from one color to another. True halftones are possible in roller printing and transfer printing but not in screen printing.

Overlays, or *fall-ons*, are overlapping color areas that are printed twice. Colors will be darker, or at least different. For instance, blue overlaid on yellow will produce a shade of green.

A *pattern repeat* is one total, complete pattern unit. A polka dot may have a one-inch-square repeat or be of mural proportions. Normally, repeats are not larger than a roller or screen, i.e., sixteen to forty-eight inches.

Penetration is the degree or depth to which the ground absorbs the dyestuff. Poor penetration may result in dry-looking areas or show up later when abrasion wears down the thinly printed layer. These problems tend to arise in cloths with ribs and valleys or with heavy nubs or lint, which resist color, then move. In more casual patterns with areas of unprinted ground such occurrences may be quite acceptable.

Pigment printing uses pigments instead of dyestuffs as colorants. After printing the pigments are cured with heat but are not given the elaborate washing and refinishing required for dyestuffs (see Part 4, section 1).

Registration is the alignment, or *fit*, of the screens or rollers that make up a pattern. Failures in alignment are referred to as *off-register*. The resulting slices of ground are called *grins*.

Selvage legend refers to self-printed copy on the selvage. Information may include the originator of the pattern, the designer, the copyright, and color blocks.

PREPRINTING PROCESSES

All cloths, whatever printing technique is used, must be *prepared* for printing. This includes scouring, shrinking, often bleaching, and, in the case of cotton, mercerizing. Some cloths even have their chemistry ("sex") changed so that they accept certain dyestuffs better.

PRINTING PROCESSES

When the authors were students, fabric printing was explained in terms of traditional block printing, the dominant roller-printing industry, and a newcomer—silk-screen printing. Today, block printing has all but expired; roller printing is almost completely relegated to children's sleepwear;

screen printing—with vast new efficiencies—dominates the market; and several old and new processes compete for market and spotlight.

Print Quality

Print quality is generally thought of in terms of a "standard product"—as dull and well-matched as Nabisco wafers. Print quality is much more: it is craft. It has compelling beauty; it is the shared testimonial of that remarkable coupling of thirsty fibers and color in a liquid dyebath. The pattern and the color are *in* the fabric, not *on* it. We know how it got there, and yet there is mystery and magic in such cloths. Many of them were made in the distant past or in distant places such as Cambodia and Sumatra.

Today, production fabrics seldom have this magical quality. Hand prints are almost without exception hand-screened. However remarkable this twentieth-century invention is, it is a production process, not a craft technique. Those of us who are dedicated to design also use it—we must. But the challenge is to overcome the simplistic banalities. There are many ways to do this. Ken Scott uses drama and chic. Pucci has a knowing, graphic ingenuity. Vuokko and Marimekko employ bombast and scale. Larsen fabrics fight back with overprinting, enormous care in coloring, and special grounds. But the unschooled Yoruba printer in Nigeria can laugh at all of us. Her five yards a week—or a month—have a quality that we cannot obtain.

Old Techniques

Even older, perhaps, than blocking or stamping a pattern on fabric are several craft-printing techniques. Except for drawing or painting directly on cloth, these are usually *reserve*, or *resist*, *prints* such as the starch resists of ancient China and wax resists, or *batiks* (see figure 4-1). The resist material is drawn, stamped, or stenciled onto the cloth; the cloth is dyed; and the resist is removed. Usually the process must be repeated for each color used. In *tie-dyes* and *fold dyes* areas of the cloth are wrapped so tightly that they resist penetration of the dyebath. *Ikats* (see figure C-11) are woven with yarns that are tied and dyed into a pattern. The patterning yarns may be in the warp, weft, or both.

These ancient resist-printing techiques have in common a phase of immersion dyeing. Resist prints first developed because they provide the best way of getting colorants into the fiber, particularly with vegetable dyes. Resist printing is seldom used today: the extra steps are less economical than direct printing methods.

Block Printing

Carved of wood or wood embedded with metal, *printing blocks* are seldom as large as a foot. Using one block for each color or pattern motif, the overall repeat may require up to a hundred blocks. Each will be loaded with dye paste, carefully positioned, then stamped onto the cloth. The time and skill required necessarily make this a preindustrial technique, and the last of the great old block-printing operations in England and France have closed down. Today, probably half of all block printing is done in India, Pakistan, and Iran. In Eastern Europe, West Africa, and Indonesia, particularly, simpler motifs are hand-blocked in resist pastes, then overdyed in indigo or another single color.

4-2. Eleven English hand blocks, each of which prints a single area, are shown here in separate impressions. (Photo courtesy Cooper-Hewitt Museum.)

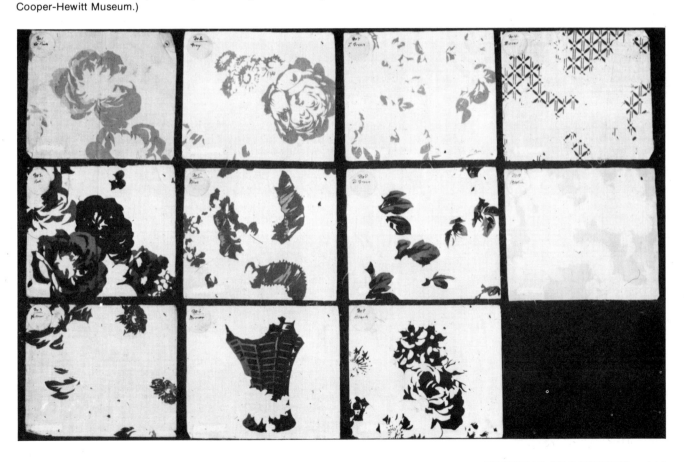

Roller Printing

Of all fabric-printing methods, *roller printing* is closest to newspaper printing. The copper rollers are engraved by hand or, more often, etched with acid to form a relief. A second, unetched cylinder rolls dye paste onto the print roller, which in turn transfers the dye to the cloth. Although a separate pair of rollers is required for each color, they print in close succession. Because the cloth moves through the printing machine only once, accurate registration is assured.

The advantages of roller printing are not only speed and economy but also the fineness of line and the shaded halftones that are made possible.

4-3. The precision and fine detailing that can be achieved by printing with engraved metal rollers is illustrated in this old fragment of French toile de Jouy. (Photo courtesy Cooper-Hewitt Museum.)

Although it is rarely utilized today, roller printing has the potential of imparting to fabric all the special qualities of etchings and line engravings. The great toiles de Jouy (see figure 4-3) testify to this.

The limitations of the technique are the short vertical repeats and the necessarily long production runs. Moreover, as roller printing has been largely relegated to cheap markets, the printers tend to be neither innovative nor particularly careful with the coloring.

Screen Printing

Screen printing is a modified stencil process. The stencil is a sheer, close-meshed fabric screen (originally silk organdy but now usually woven filament nylon or polyester), which is stretched tightly over a large wood or metal frame; areas not to be printed are blocked out to form a pattern-making stencil.

In *hand*, or *table*, *printing* the cloth is secured to the top of a bed or table, usually fifty yards long. The screen is positioned, or *registered*, on the cloth, and dye paste is pushed through the screen by means of a heavy rubber blade called a *squeegee*. The screen is then lifted to the next position, and the process is repeated. Each color of the pattern has its own screen, so for a twelve-color hand print the process would be repeated twelve times. Still, compared with weaving, production is quite rapid and very flexible. Short runs are possible, and trials or strike-offs are only of nuisance proportions, as both start-up and change-over time are at a minimum.

Automatic, *machine-screen*, or *Buser printing* is similar to the above in that the principle is the same and the cloth is still horizontal. The motions, however, are all mechanized for speed and accuracy, and the cloth—not the screens—moves forward on a wide conveyor belt.

In *rotary-screen printing* the print cloth moves under a series of large cylinders. Each cylinder is a "silk screen"; each controls one color and one pattern area. Since its inception in the 1960s rotary-screen printing, in the large middle-priced market, has eclipsed other screen-printing methods. It is extremely fast and very accurate in registration. Whereas there are set limits to the size of the repeat, they are not so short as in roller printing, nor are the production minimums so large. Continuous vertical stripes are among the unique possibilities. Short runs and strike-offs are problematic.

Transfer Printing

Transfer printing, also called *heat-transfer printing* or *Sublistatic printing*, utilizes the principle of the decal. The pattern is printed with disperse dyes on a waxed paper. When it is transferred onto cloth under heat and pressure, these dyes actually *sublime*—pass from a solid into a gaseous state— and are absorbed into the fibers. But because all transfer prints to date use disperse dyes that have an affinity only for certain synthetic fibers, the process is somewhat limited.

Transfer printing often lacks intensity and depth of shade. On the plus side this method can, like color lithography, reproduce all the halftone shadings and nuances of watercolors and photographs. Although preparing the paper for transfer printing now requires considerable lead time and sizable minimums, the transfer can be made quickly on compact equipment, in small quantities, and without washing or refinishing. Moreover, transfer paper is sufficiently compact for easy storage and transcontinental shipment. In the future there will be more transfer printing.

Other Printing Techniques

Discharge printing is done by discharging or bleaching out areas of color from a dyed cloth. The cloth may be yarn-dyed, but it is usually piece-dyed with dischargeable dyes. Prints may be *discharged-to-ground*, as above, or *discharge-and-print*. In the latter case vat dyes are mixed with a discharging chemical, and color is simultaneously removed and replaced with another shade. This method is especially useful for printing large areas of dark or colored grounds. It also has a special quality, with characteristic halos around color areas. With each new lot you should expect shade variations from the original sample, as the color is hard to control.

In *resist*, or *reserve*, *printing*, as opposed to the usual *direct printing* of color on cloth, pattern areas are *reserved* by applying a wax or paste resist. The cloth is then dyed, and the resist removed. Because this means three processes instead of one, resist printing is being phased out of normal production. In direct printing a partial resist is sometimes printed under areas to be overprinted with dye. The effect may be softly haloed or a sharp, frothy white.

Etching, or *burn-out printing*, is rather similar to discharge printing. The cloth, not the color, is removed by a printed acid. Usually, the ground is woven of a basic polyester voile with a supplementary warp or weft of a heavier, cellulosic yarn. When the cellulosic yarns are "burned" away, the sheer voile remains. Self-toned opaque, transparent patterns are effective, and both the voile and the denser areas may be printed with color (see figure 4-4). We will see more variations in etching techniques, including removal of the total weft to expose areas of unengaged warp. Another variation, *hole-out printing*, removes *all* the cloth with lifesaverlike holes.

Flock prints are made by printing areas of adhesive onto a ground, which is then sprayed with *flock*, or short, chopped rayon, nylon, or other fibers. The resultant surface is similar to a dense velvet. In *electrostatic flocking* the fibers are electrically charged. This process makes the fibers stand bolt upright, like steel filings on a magnet. With either method the performance and cleaning characteristics of flock prints will only be as good as the adhesive employed. If no cleaning instructions are given, ask for them.

Warp printing is direct printing onto the beamed warp yarns before the cloth is woven. The effect is shadowy and integrated.

In *plissé prints* the printed areas are shrunk to form a blistered surface, which may or may not be permanent. Striped "seersuckers" are typical cloths, but others are possible.

There is also a new wave of programmed printing techniques, in which color is dipped onto wet cloth (see figure 4-5) or shot through hundreds of hollow needles. Expect the impossible!

4-4. *Oberon*, an etched print, achieves its unique quality by first weaving a two-layered cloth of cotton satin superimposed on polyester voile. The field, or blotch, is then printed with acid, and the cotton burned out to expose the filmy voile.

Like gold, diamonds, a lady's company, and other prizes, the glories of color do not come without travail. Frankly, problems still plague everyone involved with color. So long as we care about special colors, innovation, custom application, or luxury materials, there will be problems of color match and colorfastness.

There are fewer problems—particularly for the designer, retailer, and consumer—with stable, mass-produced goods. Runs are larger, produced longer in advance, and with more controls and testing. Shades that cause problems are weeded out; if necessary, brilliance is sacrificed in favor of stability.

Unlike apparel fabrics, furnishings fabrics have some special problems. Although many of them are never laundered or exposed to bleaches or perspiration, their exposure to light is constant and unrelenting. The need for solutions to fastness problems is at a peak. Even more problematic are decorative fabrics sold from samples, often several years old. Selection is necessarily from one lot, delivery from another (see Part 2, section 2).

Luxury fabrics are produced in small lots. Their technology is often at the extreme edge of feasibility. More and more often their production is foreign and exotic. The challenge to fabric house, designer, and consumer is to steer a course between the too safe and the foolhardy. Of course, there is always a place for fabrics that are too safe and even for those that entail extravagant risks. Be sure you have such a place and something to compensate for either the dullness or the possibility of replacement before you make your selection.

Of all interior furnishings, fabrics are the most variable in color and the most difficult to control. If the color of a specific fabric is important, such as a dominant pattern that conditions the choice of paint and carpet, it is prudent to secure the actual fabric early and match to *it*, *not* to a sample from a previous dye lot.

4-5. The Ambiente process, invented by Timo Saarpaneva of Finland, heralds postindustrial craftsmanship. The design is printed on wet cloth on both sides simultaneously; a computerized robot spreads color or vacuums it out. The marriage of dye and fiber, the directness of the designing, and the finesse of the graduated halftones are quite close to the fold-dyed fabric shown in figure C-12.

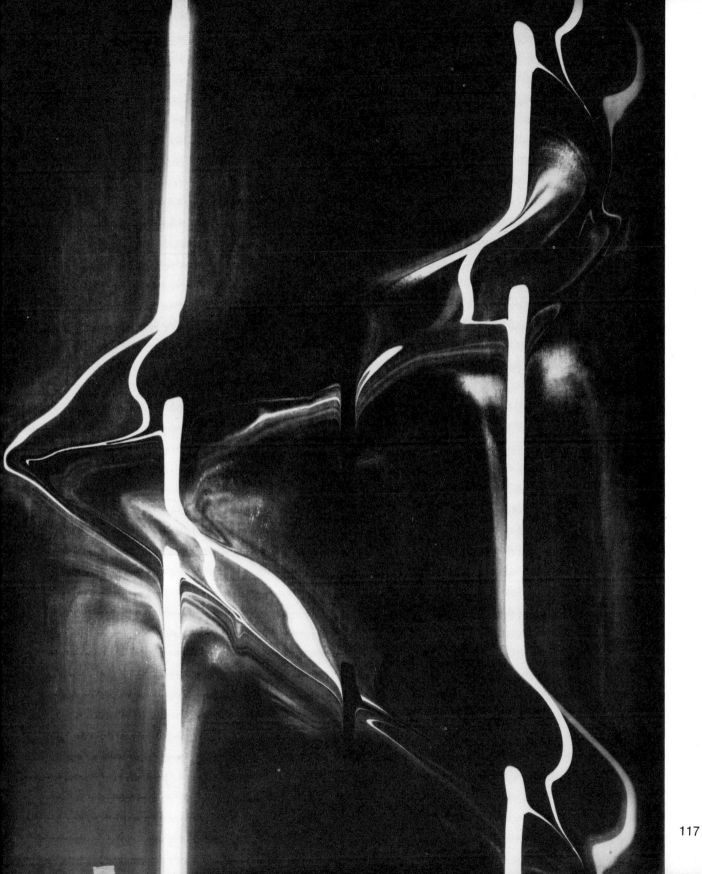

PART 5: PROFESSIONAL PRACTICE

This short section attempts to highlight some general information that should be available to everyone working with furnishings fabrics. It covers safeguards, custom services, a brief description of the industry, and budgeting.

5-1. An ingenious use of fabric on shutters and blinds provides this room with three pattern and color changes. With the shutters closed, crisply delineated arches warm a white wall. With the shutters fully opened, a fabric print of polychrome dots covers the wall, including the venetian blinds. The blinds themselves can be flipped to a single, solid color.

1. Safeguards

The best safeguard against mistakes is an open-minded, knowledgeable understanding of fabric, including the elementary facts and relationships set forth in this handbook. Asking questions helps; so does reading labels and fact sheets—particularly if they contain disclaimers. Frankness is professional at all times, as is sufficient reliance on common sense to know that newer is not necessarily better, or a costly fabric durable and carefree, or an inexpensive fabric a bargain (see Part 5, section 4). Salespeople tend to emphasize the virtues of a product. It is reasonable to ask for its limitations— "Where should I *not* use it?" Don't ask if it is "residential" or "contract," but where, specifically, it is to be used and how it should be maintained. A few standards help: they are listed here.

TESTING

Testing varies considerably: from free and immediate to slow and costly; from positive to conclusive to relative tendencies; from a normal part of production to requirements for specific codes or installations. On all levels testing is on the upswing.

Hand tests are simple, free, and immediate. Some, like those for fiber identification, are conclusive; others only raise further questions. The simple *burn test* is useful: cotton and viscose burn quickly with a powdery ash and a noticeable smell of burning paper; protein fibers burn more slowly with a crisp ash and a smell of burning hair or feathers; and synthetic fibers tend to melt with a beady ash. It is important to remember, however, that this test is for identification only, not for flame retardance. In testing for the latter the question is not burning but whether the fabric will support a flame after the match is removed. A hand test may suggest yes or no, but a lab test is required to pass codes and to obtain such specifics as flame spread (see below).

The old test for linen was absorbency, but wrinkle-resistant resin finishes also defy moisture. A professional can taste the sourness of silk and feel the stiffness of hemp. He will crush a fabric in his palm to see if it will bounce back. Creasing a fabric between thumb and forefinger is also common, as is stretching the middle section of a swatch and noting the degree of "return." Fuzzing and pilling may be checked with a downward, rotary movement of the forefinger. Pile loss may be checked by attempting to pull tufts out from the face or to rub them out from the back with a pencil eraser. Most fabrics will lose some pile, but it is the amount of loss that is critical (see Part 3, section 4). Raveling, slip resistance, and crocking can be tested by hand (see Part 2, section 2). Bleeding can be checked by compressing a wet swatch between two layers of dry cotton or tissue.

Hang tests, although they require more fabric, are simple and depend only on common sense and experience. They are usually used for window fabrics, and there are two kinds. Unhemmed lengths at least eight or nine feet long are hung to check shrinking or elongation. They are most accurate if performed in the climatic—especially humidity—conditions that prevail in the installation location (see Part 2, section 1). To check for light control, transparency, draping quality, and stacking, hang tests (often comparative) are made with fabric lengths or made-up draperies. The same lengths can and should be used for cleaning tests.

Cleaning tests to determine the type of cleaning required are usually made by the producer, converter, or fabric house. Shrinkage and loss of appearance or finish are especially checked.

Fading tests are sometimes performed to check color loss in washing or dry cleaning, but this is infrequent nowadays. These tests are usually included in the cleaning tests mentioned above. Occasionally fabrics, especially dyed acetate, are tested for gas fading (see Part 4, section 1). Normally, however, fading tests are run for fastness to light. For many decades the standard test has been exposure to ultraviolet light at a specific humidity. This is done with a machine called a *Fade-Ometer*, which indicates color loss at intervals of twenty Fade-Ometer hours. For luxury furnishing fabrics forty hours is considered barely adequate. For carpets, wall coverings, and goods sold over the counter eighty hours is sought. More and more frequently color loss is being measured by an international scale which grades fabrics from one to eight. Four is adequate, and five to six is sought. Remember, however, that there may be wide variations within one multicolored fabric or from one color to the next. There may also be considerable variation from one dye lot to another.

Color may also be tested by clocked exposure to actual sunlight. As this process is both slow and expensive, it is not in common use.

Wear tests for abrasion resistance in upholstery fabrics are most often performed by the *Taber* and *Wyzenbeek* methods. (The *Martindale* method favored in Europe is similar to the Wyzenbeek.) Because the Taber is more elementary and faster, it is less expensive—both in terms of purchasing the machine and of performing the test. A circle of fabric is clamped on a revolving platform and exposed to the action of two abrasive wheels. The test is measured by the number of revolutions required to break, or fracture, a yarn. The results, measured in hundreds of revolutions, vary with the amount of pressure or weight applied and with the caliber of the grit.

With the Wyzenbeek method the fabric is rubbed back and forth by a cloth-covered roller. Double rubs are measured in thousands. Normally, the fabric is tested in both warp and filling directions, and fifteen thousand double rubs is considered good. Both testing methods are relative and do not correspond exactly to actual wear. The Taber test, especially, seems unfair to fine yarns and satin constructions, but such errors are on the conservative or safe side.

Fire retardance or *flame resistance* is measured in several ways. The method most frequently used by testing laboratories is to first stretch the fabric at a forty-five-degree angle, then to clock the seconds that elapse before the ignited fabric self-extinguishes. Another method measures the area of flame spread. Still another times the afterglow. Fumes are also checked and rated in *toxicity tests*. Some codes require passing grades in two or three such tests, often after a specified number of washings or cleanings. At this writing only wall coverings and floor coverings are occasionally required to pass the crucial, expensive *Tunnel test*. This test (ASTM E-84), generally specified by fire-rating codes, measures the rate of flame spread, the amount of heat absorbed by a material before it will ignite, and the smoke density. Results are scored on a scale of zero to one hundred, and an A rating is given if scores in all three categories are below twenty-five.

Other tests include resistance to bacteria and insect attack; tensile strength, which is seldom critical in furnishing fabrics; crocking; and shading coefficients.

FLAWS AND FAULTS

This section has not been inserted to make the fabric buyer even less tolerant of inconsistencies within a cloth. We have already witnessed a century of overrefining fabric in order to achieve a fault-free but sterile "standard product." The purpose is rather to provide a common language for vendor and client.

A *flaw* is an inconsistency within a fabric. Some flaws are mendable or otherwise correctable during inspection. Others are sufficiently serious to be tagged, and a compensating allowance made. Standards vary with end use and market, but a certain number of tagged flaws within a piece will qualify it as a *second*. What might count as flaws in commercial goods may be essential or at least unavoidable in handcrafted fabrics. The standard becomes the "consistency of inconsistencies"; streaks or bars that are more or less constant throughout a piece must be considered acceptable.

A *fault* is an eccentric characteristic of an entire piece or lot of fabric. A fault may be a mechanical weakness that disqualifies a cloth from its intended use or a variation in color shade. In other words, a faulty fabric may be better or more beautiful than the standard, but different. Flaws and faults are specified in several ways. Those occurring in fabric construction are referred to as *mechanical*. Some of these are listed below (see also Part 4, sections 1 and 2).

A *bar, barr, barré, or bar mark*, the most frequent visual flaw, is a horizontal band varying in width from a single pick (usually referred to as a heavy or a light pick) to the width of an entire yarn bobbin (two to six inches). If two or more shuttles are intermixed on a plain fabric, the flaw may appear as a succession of horizontal lines. Bars may be caused by variations in yarn size, color, or texture or by uneven positioning of the yarn. Some handwoven fabrics are so consistently barred that the "defect" is a hallmark.

Broken warp ends occur frequently but are usually mended before shipment. Sometimes a broken end on the loom will engage other ends, causing a serious complex of mispicks and warp floats. If such a flaw cannot be mended, it is tagged, and an allowance made.

Fly is yarn contamination caused by another bit of color or fiber intruding during the spinning process or by lint trapped in the fabric during construction. If it is slight, it can be picked out with a needle.

A horizontal and/or vertical *warp float* occurs when a warp end does not interlace with the filling yarn. Very short floats are often harmless and acceptable. Longer floats are mended with a needle. A filling float is generally termed a *mispick*.

A *hole* in weaving is a major flaw, generally the result of a *smash* caused by the beater crashing down on a shuttle trapped in the warp. In warp knits a hole is the result of a broken end and is easily mended.

Small *knots* or knots in a heavily textured fabric may be harmless, especially if they are pushed to the reverse side. Larger knots are untied on the mending table and darned into the fabric. They may also be corrected by the upholsterer or in the workroom.

A *reed mark* is a vertical streak caused by a bent wire in the reed, or comb.

A *skip pick* is a missing shot of filling that extends all or partway across the cloth. It is usually caused by a bobbin running out of yarn. In a plain weave it results in two filling yarns running as one.

Short or *tight selvages* or the reverse, *long selvages*, if intermittent, may be a flaw. If they are consistent, they may or may not be a fault. In lightweight goods the selvage tends to be tight. At other times it is so full or long that it has a slight ripple. Either condition may be revealed only in hanging, with a change of humidity, or after cleaning. For this reason selvages are not used but cut off. Sometimes, as a shortcut in drapery making, the selvages are merely *clipped*, i.e., cut with scissors at intervals of twelve inches or more after seaming. If a tight or loose selvage is many inches wide, the condition may be serious. An upholsterer can usually correct the situation. In fabrics for windows and walls correction is possible only if the damage is slight. A pattern or horizontal stripe aggravates the problem.

A *slub* is an exceptionally heavy area within a yarn. It may occur in either a warp or a filling.

A *slug* is a loose filling that loops in and out of

the cloth. It is mendable by darning or by pulling the slack to the selvage.

Burrs and other vegetable materials most often occur in hand-spun wools that are neither graded nor carbonized to dissolve them. As they may readily be picked out at any time, this is not a permanent problem. Similarly, some cottons may contain bits of cottonseed, or silk may hold fragments of larva shell.

Dirt or *grease* is usually removed in scouring. In loom-state goods it is normally removed or tagged during inspection. It is most apt to occur at the end of a piece.

Off-grain is usually a finishing fault in which the horizontal yarns run at an angle. If it is slight or in plain goods, it may not be a problem. Striped patterns are the least tolerant: a damaged order should be returned for refinishing.

Pile loss can occur during printing, dyeing, or finishing. It may be inoffensively slight or an uncorrectable fault.

Slippage, or warp yarns sliding on the filling, sometimes occurs in finishing.

Tender goods refers to fabric that has lost its tensile strength because of heat or chemicals. The condition is rare but dangerous.

SPECIFICATION AND PURCHASE ORDERS

It is sound practice to put all orders in writing and sign them. If an order is verbal, a written confirmation should follow. A purchase-order number helps in tracing and in preventing duplication—or the seller's assumption of duplication. A separate purchase order for each item is often useful.

The purchase order must contain the buyer's name and address, plus phone, cable, and Telex address, if any. If the billing address is different, it should be so stated. The shipping address should be stated, even if it is the same as the letterhead. The purchase order should indicate that the shipment is *marked for* a specific assignment. The best markings are specific enough to help prevent errors at the workroom. They state not only who the job is for but also what the job is.

The method of shipping and the shipping date required should be indicated. "Rush" written on all

orders becomes meaningless. More sensible specifications are: "Notify immediately if shipment cannot be made by such and such a date," "Will accept partial shipment," or "Hold for shipping instructions." On a corporate purchase order or an order from a buyer other than the specifier, the specifier's name and firm should be indicated; if a designer's approval is required, it will then be directed to the right person. (Sales personnel will also be properly credited.)

With problematic deliveries and fluctuating prices it has become good practice to check stock and price by telephone, place the order "on reserve," and then send in the signed purchase order. Requesting a swatch from the actual lot to be cut is reasonable. A swatch from "current stock" is not; if there is no reserve, that stock may be depleted at any given moment.

The actual purchase is stated in terms of number of yards (decorative fabrics are usually calculated in eighths or quarters) and the number, name, *and* color of the design. This seeming redundancy is your insurance against error. The unit price is stated, and the extension made.

Cuts, or allowable unit lengths, should be specified for both window and wall fabrics. This is often in the form of a footnote, such as: "Required: nineteen cuts (or panels) nine feet long." The shipping room will then try to make sure that the necessary cuts are sent. With large orders the yardage requirements of each room or unit should be given— with instructions that each room or unit must be cut from the same lot.

2. Custom Services

In addition to the tens of thousands of fabrics that are distributed as "in stock" and ready for use, there are still facilities for custom or customized design and for modification through special finishes or aftertreatments. Full custom design is less common today than in the thirties and forties, partly because of the wider range and higher quality of in-stock fabrics and the larger, more remote production centers. The most flexible areas are custom carpets. hand-woven blinds and fabrics—mostly from California producers—and custom printing.

Particularly for very large, monumental installations or for corporate or institutional identification programs, custom design should be considered—and often a fabric-design consultant as well. In addition to fabric houses that specialize in custom work, many other houses are prepared—with a sufficiently high minimum and enough lead time—to deliver custom or customized design. In woven fabrics the easiest changes are on standard warps woven through with stocked wefts. Certain classes of piece-dyed fabrics can be custom-colored with satisfactory fastness and in reasonable minimums.

In screen prints custom color is not uncommon, especially with designs requiring a few screens and pigment colors. Custom-print houses usually offer a choice of ground cloths as well.

There are instances in which the justification for custom design or custom color should be questioned. Certain risks exist, especially with commissioning, i.e., buying before seeing. Most fabric designing goes through a long evolutionary phase; bypassing or short-cutting this weeding out and selecting process in order to create a "sport" should be questioned—especially if the only reason for a custom route is to satisfy the vanity of the designer or his client. In any case testing and quality control are less possible, and returns are impossible. Specifications and purchase orders should be for the protection of both buyer and seller, contractual and signed. In no case should the delay and expense of approving a strike-off be dispensed with.

Special finishes are readily and inexpensively available on a custom basis. Flame-retardant, soil-resistant, and latex- or acrylic-backing finishes are the most common. Antibacterial finishes, plastic coating, and mothproofing are also available, as are plasticizing and plastic lamination—but from different processors.

Although special finishers and custom dyers are concentrated in such regional hubs as New York, Chicago, and Los Angeles, they tend to work nationally. Send purchase orders to fabric houses with instructions to ship to a special finisher. Another purchase order, directed to the finisher, specifies the finish or treatment desired and the shipping and billing instructions.

Other processes, such as backings for wall coverings (see Part 2, section 3) or quilting, are handled in much the same way. Just remember to make the directions clear and specific. Most processors have price lists and brochures that describe their services. Use the specific trade names listed. If there are specific requirements or deadlines, state them. When necessary, have tests made.

———————————>

C-9. Each of these four brilliant casement panels is shaded across its width—from yellow to orange, orange to magenta, purple to blue-green, and green to yellow. The sequence may simply follow the spectrum; longer repeats may be composed; or one or two colors may be used. Inverting alternate panels doubles the repeat. The translucent plain-woven woolen cloth is interrupted with heavier stripes of glossy, worsted satin weave to create contrasts in texture and opacity.

C-10. True iridescence is most likely to occur when yarns are fine and of high luster. Few cloths have more fire than these Bangalore silks, in which the fine warps complement the heavier weft in value and color.

Woven fabrics have an extraordinary potential for reproducing scintillating broken colors. The scale of the yarn and pattern and the closeness of color values are key factors.

C-11. An Irish jacquard, also shown in detail in figure 3-24. The three colors vary in intensity as well as hue.

C-12. This closeup of a striped double plain weave in Irish wool illustrates the fusion possible with close values and analogous colors.

C-13. Laotian Ikat obtains its character from the richness of the gold silk yarns and the mélange of tropical colors.

C-14. To create a shimmering, rich surface, a weft-faced pattern weave combines a dozen yarns of various weights and textures and of analogous tonalities.

C-9.

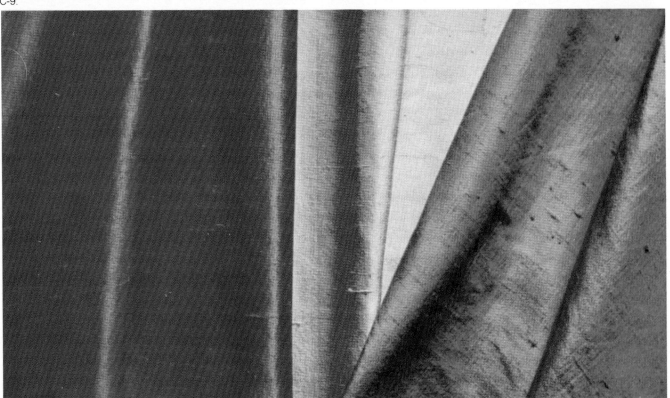

C-10.

C-12. ▲

C-13. ▼

C-14. ▼

3. The Fabric Industry

Fabric is the oldest industry—that is, the first to undergo industrialization. In the United States fabric—together with related soft goods—is also the largest industry. The fabric industry has two relatively new but increasingly powerful allies. One is the small number of sizable firms who produce man-made fibers. Many of them also make dyestuffs and the chemicals, resins, and adhesives used in fabric finishing. Today, these firms are an integral and increasingly visible aspect of the fabric complex. The other ally is natural-fiber producers, who, if slow in entering the fray, have learned that they too are part of the fabric world, and they are investing in research and in industrial and consumer relations.

The fabric industry is in flux—indeed, in the first stages of a second industrial revolution. Production is more and more automated and rationalized. The fabrication of textile consumer goods will undergo upheaval as well—with unsettling, open-ended consequences. Distribution will undoubtedly follow the new suit.

Within this giant (but not at all unilateral) complex, the segment involved with interiors is small, perhaps as little as ten percent of the total in the United States and very much lower in less developed countries. These furnishings fabrics are produced by giant mills and textile conglomerates, by middle-sized producers, and by small specialists ranging from a staff of a hundred or so to a single independent craftsman. Producers of all sizes are divided not only by market and end use and by price or class but also by horizontal versus vertical operation. A *horizontal operation*, such as a cotton gray-goods mill, is involved with one aspect of production and may sell to a variety of users. A *vertical operation* may start with fiber or yarn but carries production through dyeing and finishing and sometimes, as with sheets and towels, even to packaging and sales distribution.

In recent years the impact of imports has created a new segment of the industry, the *import house*. Whether they are in the form of gray goods, finished cloth, or consumer goods, imports are now a major aspect of American fabrics.

To summarize, the whole fabric field is in a state of growth and flux, not only in terms of new fibers and finishes but of production, styling, and distribution. Product lines have been greatly expanded, with broader variety in both contemporary and traditional patterns. As large firms have grown larger, small sources for specialty fabrics have sprung up. Exotic imports styled for the American market are more common and more broadly distributed.

CONVERSION

Fabric *conversion* encompasses a broad array of specialized technology. It is a growing industry and a trend of industrial proportions: it includes all postconstruction processes—finishing, dyeing, printing, and an expanding number of special techniques. (It does not include standard finishes by a prime producer such as a woolen mill.)

Converting arose as an industry when cotton dominated the market. Northern converters bought up cotton gray goods from provincial mills, assuming the risks of styling and market fluctuation and the responsibility for dyeing, printing, and finishing. The converter of furnishings fabrics distributed to jobbers, retailers, and the cutting-up trades.

Today, the converter still does all this—and more. He usually commissions yarn-dyed goods as well, and his range of fibers and cloths has expanded laterally. Often, he produces ready-made draperies, bedspreads, and cushions. He may have merged with a textile conglomerate, or, like Burlington House, he may be an outgrowth of a corporate structure.

But fabric conversion is larger, more important, and more widespread than the converters as a specialized industry. Conversion involves the major, worldwide trend to produce large quantities of unspecialized fabrics, then to convert these gray goods into cloths that are particular, exclusive, and timely. The goal is true mass production of common-denominator commodities—in the sense that wheat and crude petroleum are commodities. The investment involved in such unspecialized goods is at a minimum: they can be freely traded on the international exchange. Production is geared not to a fickle, fluctuating market but to the needs of the producing system. Usually this means nonstop, continuous grinding out of as few different cloths as possible. Five hundred looms in one shed, weaving the same cloth, eighteen shifts a week, automated by a handful of personnel—this is production. *Conversion is the process that changes this bland, monotonous stuff into cloths that are special enough to be salable and profitable.*

The principle is pervasive. It embraces most soft goods—piece-dyed and printed carpets are a newer extension. Because it is economically sound, conversion will spread into more and more areas of consumer goods. To summarize the advantages: (1) mass production is at peak; (2) the large inventories are at their most flexible; (3) international tariffs are at the lowest, "unfinished-goods" rates; (4) conversion techniques can be in small enough quantities to provide exclusivity; (5) conversion techniques can provide much faster delivery than production starting with yarn and loom preparation; (6) conversion techniques can move in step with rapid changes in fashion and style; (7) in short, styling and merchandising decisions are as close as possible to the point of sale.

While the ingenuity of present-day pattern makers, stylists, and colorists is indeed remarkable—often genuinely creative and sometimes a delight to both eye and mind—conversion is by definition cosmetically superficial. It is to be hoped that we shall never have *only* converted fabrics.

JOBBERS

Traditionally, the fabric *jobber* is a merchant who buys job, or production, lots from the producer or converter. He then inventories and samples his goods and sells to his customers in smaller yardages within the delivery time they require. The lots that the jobber buys may be fully converted or finished under his guidance. The jobber's single orders to the converter are almost always multiple bolts of fabric—sometimes in tens or hundreds of thousands of yards. The jobber generally sells *piece goods*, i.e., one or more bolts or pieces of fabric, to his customers, who in turn sell *cut orders*, i.e., specific yardages cut to order from the bolt.

In the decorative-fabric field today, the converter and jobber may be one and the same or, for various product lines, fulfill one or both functions.

The regional jobber's function is to stock samples and distribute fabrics in local markets—primarily those servicing local retailers, furniture manufacturers, and decorator shops. In this sense he still works fairly rigidly within the traditional scope of jobbing. Of necessity, his stock is usually restricted to the popular, middle-priced lines.

FABRIC HOUSES

As the roles of producer, converter, jobber, and importer intermingle, it becomes easier to refer to them collectively as *fabric houses*. Some fabric houses specialize in particular aspects of production, price, or design; some are generalists. Fabric houses are classified according to their type of customer, which usually corresponds to their location as *downtown* (Manhattan), *uptown* (Manhattan), or *regional*.

In the decades since World War II fabric houses have been merging at an accelerating rate. Although more and more uptown and downtown houses have become divisions of the giant firms headquartered on New York's Avenue of the Americas, their showrooms, both national and regional, have tended to remain in established showroom areas. Stronger regional showrooms have been built up, partly because the residential and contract markets have grown and fewer retailers stock decorative fabrics. The major showroom areas now include Chicago, Los Angeles, San Francisco, Seattle, Dallas, Atlanta, Miami, and Boston. More are coming.

The downtown house generally sells to retailers and furniture manufacturers, as well as to the uptown and out-of-town, or regional, houses. A number of these downtown firms sell ready-made curtains, draperies, and bedspreads. Some have contract departments specializing in very large institutional and hotel work.

The uptown fabric house sells cut orders *to the trade*, that is, to (1) professional interior designers and architects; (2) special-order interior-decorating and contract departments of retail stores; and (3) furniture manufacturers who in turn sell to the trade. In other words, uptown houses are the decorative-fabric showrooms. In these showrooms fabrics are always sold through samples. The showrooms may be *open* or *closed* to consumers. "Open" means that the consumer may come unaccompanied to browse but cannot purchase. Some showrooms discourage the unattended consumer.

4. Fabric Costs and Budgeting

To get the most for his fabric investment, the buyer must understand the factors that determine the price of each fabric. In staple fabrics such as bed sheets price is determined with almost mathematical accuracy by such quality factors as fiber, fineness of yarn, closeness of weave, fabric width, and colorfastness, plus the size of the production run.

In decorative fabrics price-determining factors vary, and inherent cloth quality is not necessarily the most important. For instance, staple goods such as sailcloth and striped ticking bear highly competitive prices because, like bed sheets, production is continuous and there are no built-in development costs.

On the other hand, fabrics from specialty houses are produced in very short runs. They boast exclusivity of design; they are sometimes handcrafted and often imported. The relatively high cost of developing, sampling, and introducing an exclusive design is reflected in the fabric's price. Exclusivity and quality are becoming increasingly rare and are necessarily expensive. Moreover, the desirability of the fabric is often in inverse proportion to its availability. Do not assume that an expensive fabric will pay for itself in long wear. It very well may, but luxury fabrics are not necessarily durable, nor are they as uniform and standardized as commodity cloths.

ESTIMATED LENGTH OF SERVICE

Budgetwise, the price of the fabric itself is not the only cost factor or even the deciding one. The real price is the total cost, including installation, divided by years of service. Workroom and upholstering costs have risen much more sharply than fabrics themselves. If replacement of the fabric in a given installation is anticipated, designer and client must bear in mind that over and above the doubled fabric cost there will inevitably be a second, higher labor cost.

If over a long period of time no change in decor is expected and hard wear is foreseen, you should invest in a quality fabric that is durable enough to assure trouble-free service. Longevity of the fabric will entail a sizable saving.

If areas of hard use demand thinking in terms of durability, little-used areas suggest a lighter hand. Many guest rooms, sitting rooms, dining rooms, and executive areas are so gently or so seldom engaged that a dramatic or even a frivolous treatment is implied. Time will not make such treatments tedious, and the light traffic will not abuse the more delicate components.

On the other hand, there are valid aesthetic and psychological reasons for a designer to choose a fragile fabric for certain calculated applications. Like a party dress, the flamboyant "fashion" fabric may more than pay its way with drama. And, like a party dress, it can be counted on to become tiresome. Strategic application of fabrics with a short life expectancy in proportion to initial cost may give the interior a lift that cannot be achieved by sober practicality. Balancing yardage requirements, cost, and durability with the need for drama and change are all integral parts of the fabric plan.

THE REAL COST

One important consideration in estimating fabric cost is fabric width. We are so accustomed to thinking in terms of lineal yards that we have stopped calculating square yards or square feet. Too often, the difference between a thirty-six-inch width, the standard forty-eight- to fifty-four-inch width, and the newer hundred-inch width is overlooked. Width has an enormous bearing on the price per square yard.

In patterned fabrics matching may be another cost factor. It can increase the yardage requirement by as much as twenty-five percent.

Because the price of the fabric itself is only a factor in its total installation cost, it is mandatory to think in terms of total *installations*, such as the upholstered chair or the treated window. The difference between a twenty-, thirty-, and forty-dollar-per-yard fabric may at first glance appear to be one hundred and fifty and two hundred percent. But consider a chair costing three hundred dollars com (customer's own material, with labor charges for the upholstering included), which requires two yards of fabric. With two yards of twenty-dollar material the chair costs three hundred and forty dollars. With packing, shipping, and handling the overall cost is approximately three hundred and seventy dollars. The same chair with a forty-dollar fabric will cost four hundred and thirty dollars delivered. The difference in the cost of the chair between the cheapest and the most expensive fabric is about ten percent, *not* two hundred percent. And if, as is probable, the twenty-dollar fabric will retain a good appearance for only half as long as the forty-dollar fabric, the long-range calculation for the expensive fabric would show a considerable saving. The aesthetic advan-

tages of the expensive, more durable fabric come scot-free.

In window fabrics it is important to bear in mind that makeup, installation, lining, and maintenance costs are the same with a cheap fabric as with an expensive one. Calculating in terms of total price—square feet of draped and installed fabric—*is* reasonable. For instance, a lined drapery with sixty yards of fabric will entail a makeup cost of approximately three hundred dollars (probably more). With delivery, track, and installation a five-dollar-per-yard drapery would probably cost about seven hundred and fifty dollars. Choosing a fabric that costs twice as much will not double the installed cost but increase it by something like thirty-five percent.

THE FABRIC SUBSIDY

One approach to budgeting is to divide the total sum allowed by the yards required and never exceed that figure. Similarly, one could decide never to indulge—or even consider—anything lavish. Either approach guarantees that you will not have a single cloth of staggering beauty or of strong emotional appeal, and either is almost certain to invoke "furniture-store" monotony. Any room budget can afford a touch of fabric that is perfectly smashing—even if it is only a pillow, wall hanging, or some other fabric accessory.

Many side chairs require so little yardage that they may be the place to indulge. The furniture that will get heavy or constant use needs a quality fabric for durability—adding a little more to the cost may secure a truly handsome cloth. The budget can be easily subsidized by relying on low-cost staples for unobtrusive installations that require big yardage. Besides, the contrast between rich cloths and simple ones is often most stimulating. Old fabrics should not be ruled out for the personal interior, and stopgap approaches sometimes breed freshness and spontaneity otherwise not planned for. The moral, of course, is that a decorative fabric is not a staple commodity but a matter of personal involvement.

It pays to shop for the best for two reasons: (1) the best inoculates the shopper against second-rate design; and (2) this approach may provide immediate proof that what you want is actually not that much more costly than what is only acceptable. This is particularly so when the real cost of the installed fabric is borne in mind. This concept may be more illuminating to the client if the designer calculates the final, overall installation cost based on two or three fabric price levels.

And, in areas where costs must be cut, remember that *economical shopping requires time*. In other words, the less money available, the more time will be required to find an acceptable fabric. The crucial question becomes, whose time? A professional interior designer's time costs (or should cost) money. If the client's time is readily available, the designer should allow him or her to visit suggested showrooms, and the client should be made aware of clearance sales, warehouse sales, etc. This requires organization. The shopper must be armed with the designer's business card and should be given color samples for the room scheme, plus exact yardage requirements.

BIBLIOGRAPHY

Emery, Irene. *The Primary Structures of Fabrics.* Textile Museum, Washington, D. C., 1966.

Encyclopedia of Textiles. Editors of American Fabrics Magazine. Prentice-Hall, Englewood Cliffs, N. J., 1972.

Joseph, Marjory L. *Introductory Textile Science.* Holt, Rinehart, and Winston, New York, 1966.

Linton, George E. The *Modern Textile Dictionary.* Textile Book Service, Plainfield, N.J., 1973.

Man-Made Fiber Fact Book. Man-Made Fiber Producers Association, Washington, D. C., 1974.

Modern Textiles. Reporter Bulletin Edition: Textile End Uses (Annual).

Pizzuto, Joseph J. *Fabric Science.* Revised by Arthur Price and Allen C. Cohen. Fairchild Publications, New York, 1974.

Textile Fibers and Their Properties. Burlington Industries, Greensboro, N. C.

Textile Organon. World Man-Made Fiber Survey (Annual). Textile Economics Bureau, New York.

PART 6: GLOSSARY-INDEX

Page references in *italics* denote illustrations. Key terms not mentioned in the text are defined here for reference.

abaca or **Manila hemp.** A fiber obtained from the leaf stalk of the banana plant. 53

abrasion resistance. Durability of a fabric in the face of surface wear. 24, 31, 32, 35, 48, 51, 58, 61, 121

Acele. Trade name of a Du Pont acetate. 58

acetate. A generic term for a man-made fiber composed of acetylated cellulose. 24, 25, 49, 57, 58, 69, 97, 108, 109, 110, 121

acid dyes. A class of dyes used primarily for protein and nylon fibers. 109

acoustical insulation. Insulation employed to reduce noise or sound. 22

Acrilan. Trade name of an acrylic fiber produced by Monsanto. 58

acrylic. A generic term for a man-made fiber composed of acrylonitrile units (at least 85 percent by weight), which are derived from petrochemical by-products. 24, 58, 98, 101, 109

additive finishes. A general term for finishes that are chemical rather than mechanical, typically used to render fabric resistant to soil, wrinkles, or flame, for example. 96

alpaca. A luxurious natural-protein fiber obtained from an Andean camelidae related to the Asiatic camel. 55, 104

Ambiente. A new printing process in which the design is applied by computer to one or both sides of a wet cloth. 116, *117*

angora. A goat native to Turkey from which mohair is obtained. 54

animal fibers. A general term that refers to all natural-protein fibers, including wool, silk, and goat hair. 50, 53, 54, 55, 68

antibacterial finishes. Chemical treatments applied to finished cloth to repel mildew and other microorganisms. 59, 98, 125

antique satin. A cloth of sateen construction with an exaggerated slub filling and a fine warp. 77

antiseptic finishes. See antibacterial finishes.

antistatic finishes. Finishes for reducing static electricity in synthetic fibers. 57

Antron. Trade name of Du Pont's trilobal-nylon fiber. 49, 58

Antron III. Trade name of Du Pont's antistatic nylon. 58

aramid. Generic term of a modified-nylon fiber. 57

Arnel. Trade name of a triacetate fiber produced by Celanese. 58

asbestos. A natural-mineral fiber primarily used for heat reduction and flame retardance. 26, 50, 109, 110

atmospheric, gas, or **fume fading.** A term used to describe color loss or change caused by gases or other pollutants. 110

Avisco. Trade name of a rayon produced by FMC.

Avril. Trade name of a high-modulus rayon produced by FMC. 58

azlon. A generic term for a man-made fiber composed of regenerated natural protein.

backfilling. A supplementary filling yarn used to pad or support a cloth.

backing. A liquid or spray plastic back coating for upholstery and wall fabrics to ensure dimensional stability or to resist slippage, raveling, or fraying. 25, 32, 34, 97, 101, 125

balanced cloth. A cloth with a symmetrical relation of vertical and horizontal elements. 22, 24, 74, 75, 76, *78*, 82

balloon cloth. A fine, densely set, plain-woven cloth of combed and carded long-staple cotton.

bangtail. A clipped weft float that forms a fringe. 88

Banlon. Trade name of a process for texturizing filament yarns licensed by Joseph Bancroft. 56

bar, barré, color bar, or **bar mark.** A flaw in which horizontal bands of darker, lighter, or different shades run from selvage to selvage. 110, 122

barathea. A twill variation with a broken rib weave on one face and a pebbly texture on the other. 75

bark cloth. (1) Nonwoven material made from soaked and beaten inner bark of tropical trees. (2) Roughly woven drapery fabric with a barklike texture. 75

basket weave. A variation of plain weave in which two or more warp ends and an equal number of weft picks are woven as one. 72, *74*, 76, *78*

bast fibers. Strong, woody fibers found in the leaves and stems of plants such as flax and jute. 51, 52

bat. A continuous sheet of fiber prepared for carding. 68

batik. A resist print in which wax is drawn or blocked onto a fabric before dyeing. *102*, 112

batiste. A fine, sheer, plain-woven cloth of combed and carded long-staple cotton.

batten, or **beater**. The movable frame on a loom that holds the comb or reed. 71

batting. Layers or sheets of fiber used for lining quilts. 21, 31, 41, 42, 70, 101

beaker dyeing. Dyeing of small samples, usually for testing purposes. 105

beam. A wood or metal cylinder attached to a loom on which the warp is wound. 71, *71*, 90, 105

beater. See batten.

beck dyeing. A method of piece dyeing small lots of fabric in an open vat, often on a custom basis, 108

Bedford cord. A weave similar to piqué in which supplementary warp ends pad a vertically channeled fabric. 10

beetling. A pounding action that flattens linen yarns to a ribbonlike profile and adds surface luster. 97

Bemberg. Trade name of a process for producing cuprammonium-rayon fibers now produced by Beaunit. 58

Berber yarn. A thick hand-spun yarn of mottled natural wool. *13*, 62, 64

Beta. Trade name of an extremely fine bulked-glass fiber with improved abrasion-resistance and flexing properties manufactured by Owens-Corning. 58

bicomponent fiber. A single fiber formed by extruding two different modifications of a polymer as one filament, usually for the purpose of building in crimp or bulk. 57

biconstituent fiber. A single fiber formed by extruding two generically different polymers as one filament. 57

bird's-eye. Traditional dobby-woven diaper pattern of concentric diamonds. A large-scale bird's-eye is called a **gooseeye**. 77, 82, 83

bleaching. The basic finishing process by which gray goods are scoured and whitened. Bleaching a fabric that has already been dyed is called **stripping**. 51, 53, 96, 104, 112, 115

bleeding. A fault in which a dyestuff runs from one pattern area into another. 109, 110, 121

blend. Combining two or more different fibers before they are spun into yarn. 57, 108

block printing. General term for a hand-printing process using wood or linoleum blocks into which patterns have been cut. 113, *113*

blooming. Bulking yarns to create a fuller, softer cloth. 96

blotch printing. An open-screen roller-printing process by which the plain background of a printed fabric can be colored. 111, *116*

bobbinet. A fine net with a six-sided mesh.

bobbin lace. A single-element construction, originally handmade on a pillow with numerous threads. 75, 76, 94, *95*

boiling off. A scouring process for fabric coming off the loom that releases grease, gum, or sizing added to yarn during production. 96

bolt. An entire length of fabric, usually rolled full-width on a tube, sometimes folded before rolling. 36, 129

bonded web. A bat of loose fiber that is compressed with heat and an adhesive material. 68

bonding. The process of laminating two fabrics or a fabric and a backing. 70, 101

bouclé. A novelty yarn that is looped to produce a pebbly surface. 50, 61, 63

bourette. An irregular, slubbed yarn or fabric made from noil silk. 55

braid. A flat or round, woven or plaited fabric used for trimming. 40, 63

broadcloth. (1) A finely woven worsted cloth that is heavily fleeced, felted and calendered to produce a lustrous finish. (2) A combed-cotton cloth woven in a fine rib weave. 50

brocade. (1) A weaving construction in which a supplementary warp and/or filling yarn is used to form a raised pattern. (2) A rich jacquard-patterned cloth in brocade weave. 16, 17, 75, 76, 88, 89

brocatelle. A satin-faced jacquard-patterned cloth in which a supplementary backing weft is used to raise the surface. 17, 52, 75, 77, 92

broché. A brocaded fabric in which underfloats are clipped mechanically, often to simulate discontinuous brocade. 88

broken color. In nature and in fabric, color that is not dull or flat but fragmented with a lively vibrancy of minute particles. 11, 13, 15, *15*, 105

broken twill. A random twill, usually woven in a 1-2-4-3 sequence. 82

brushing. A finishing process in which fibers are raised to obscure the construction of a fabric. 97

buckram. A sleazy plain-woven cotton fabric stiffened with sizing.

budgeting. 131

bulking. Plumping up filament yarns to increase their loft. 50, 56, 57

burlap. A plain-woven cloth of retted single-ply jute. 52

burling. The removal of extraneous substances such as knots, loose threads, or burrs from woven fabric.

burn-out, or **etch**, **printing**. A printing process in which an opaque or translucent pattern is produced by applying acid to a supplementary area of a fabric, usually made of a fiber separate from the ground cloth. 100, 115, 116

Buser printing. A system for automatic, flat-bed screen printing on fabric. 114

cable ply. Yarn made by twisting six or more strands to form a round section. 52, *61*, 81

Cadon. Trade name of an antistatic nylon produced by Monsanto. 58

calendering. A standard finishing process in which a cloth is pressed heavily or repeatedly under a steel roller to produce a polished surface. 90, 97

camel's hair. A fiber obtained from the undercoat of the Asiatic camel. 55

cane. A grass or reed fiber. 31, 53

canvas. A dense cloth, originally cotton, in twill or plain weave. 8, 9, 72, 76, 105

Caprolan. Trade name of a texturized-nylon fiber produced by Allied Chemical. 58

carbonizing. A finishing process that destroys vegetable matter in wool cloth, 96, 123

carding. The process of disentangling and equalizing the distribution of fiber material before spinning it into yarn. 50, 54, 64

casement cloth. A general term for sheer drapery fabric. 20, 21, 25

cashmere. A fine fiber obtained from the undercoat of the Himalayan Kashmir goat. 54, 55

cationic dyeing. A piece-dyeing process in which yarns of a single generic fiber are modified to accept different dyes and thus simulate yarn-dyed goods. 109

cavalry twill. A fancy steep twill, originally worsted, which produces a tightly woven cloth.

Celanese. Trade name of acetate yarns produced by Celanese. 58

cellulose. Organic fibrous substance found in all vegetation that is the basic constituent of both natural and man-made

cellulosic fibers such as cotton, linen, jute, and rayon. 25, 49, 57, 58, 109

chain stitch. An ornamental stitch resembling the links of a chain. 95, 99, 101

challis. A sheer, plain-woven, lightly brushed fabric of woolen, worsted, or similar-textured man-made yarns.

check. A pattern in squares. 16

cheesecloth. See tobacco cloth.

chemical, or **wet**, **finishes**. Functional finishes in which immersion is involved. 97

chenille. (1) A woven yarn or a fabric woven of this yarn. (2) A tufted cut-pile fabric, 61, 63, 90, 99

cheviot. A heavy, napped twill cloth. 75

chevron. A herringbone weave in a zigzag, diagonal pattern.

chiffon. A sheer fabric, especially of silk. 72

China grass. Ramie, particularly in an unretted form. 52

chintz. A glazed-cotton fabric, with or without a printed pattern, produced by applying resin and calendering. 28, 46, 97

Chromspun. Trade name of a solution-dyed acetate-filament yarn manufactured by Eastman.

ciré. A high-luster glaze on silk, cotton, or synthetics, produced with wax or resins and hot rollers. 97

cleaning. (1) Dry: immersion of fabric in petroleum or synthetic solvents to remove oil or grease. (2) Wet: the removal of water-borne soil or stains by a soap-and-water process, usually with a brush on a flat surface (as opposed to laundering by immersion). 22, 24, 35, 97

cloth. A useful general term for all pliable planes. 8, 25, 30, 32, 48, 50, 71, 76, 77, 84, 93, 96, 97, 98, 99, 100, 108, 111, 114, 115, 129

cloth count. The number of warp ends plus the number of filling picks in an inch or centimeter of cloth. 46, 64, 70, 75

coated fabric. A general term for a woven or knitted fabric coated usually with vinyl or other polymers, such as oilcloth and Naugahyde. 97, 101

coir. A coarse and extremely durable fiber obtained from the outer husk of coconuts. 52, 104

color abrasion. The potential loss of color, particularly in pigment prints or from poor dye penetration. 33, 52

color effects. 12, 13, 14

colorfastness. A general term denoting the relative durability of dye or pigment coloration to exposure to light, pollutants, or crocking and to laundering and cleaning processes. 110

color flag. A series of swatches attached to a sample to show the complete color line.

color line. The range of available colors of a solid or printed fabric.

color way. One individual coloration from the full color line.

color value. The lightness or darkness of a color. 21

COM. Customer's own material. 35, 132

comb. See reed.

combination dyeing. A general term that refers to a dyeing process involving cloth made of two or more different fibers. 108

combination filament yarn. A yarn composed of two or more different filaments. 57

combing. The process of laying long fibers parallel after carding and before spinning to produce a stronger, more lustrous yarn. 50, 54

compound cloths. Cloths layered in two or more thicknesses. 46, 76, 84, 99

construction. The order of interlacing of a fabric utilizing yarns or yarnlike elements. 8, 16, 17, 25, 26, 31, 32, 33, 46, 47, 48, 49, 69, 71, 82, 90, 93, 99, 105

continuous brocade. A fabric in which areas of weft are woven from selvage to complete a pattern. 76, 88

conversion. A broad array of postproduction processes, such as finishing, dyeing, printing, embroidering, or embossing, which change the basic appearance of a fabric to make it more specialized. 17, 99, 103, 104, 129

cord fabric. A general term that refers to a fabric with a pronounced horizontal or vertical rib. 30

corduroy. A cut-pile fabric, usually cotton, in which the ribbed pile is produced with a supplementary filling yarn. 10, 36, 76, 90, 91

core. A base yarn which is wrapped with a second and sometimes a third yarn element. 61, 64

core twist. A texturized stretch-yarn sheath around a fine-denier elastomeric-spandex core.

coronizing. A process in which foreign material is burned out of fiberglass fabric and the fiber is heat-set for stability and abrasion resistance.

cotton. A natural cellulosic seed-hair fiber. 24, 25, 33, 35, 48, 49, 50, 51, 52, 60, 63, 68, 72, 90, 97, 98, 104, 108, 112, 120, 129

cotton system. A spinning process, originally developed for cotton, in which very short fibers are spun to simulate various textures. 60

course. The horizontal element in a knitted fabric.

cramming. A process in which extra warp or filling yarns are forced into a cloth. 78, 79, 79, 80

crash. A low-end cloth of slubby single-ply linen, cotton, or synthetic yarn.

crepe. (1) A yarn that is overtwisted to create a crinkled profile and stretchy resilience. (2) A fabric woven of crepe yarn, which has a mat surface texture and slight stretch characteristics. 53, 64, 75

Creslan. Trade name of an acrylic fiber produced by American Cyanamid. 58

cretonne. A plain-woven printed cloth similar to unglazed chintz.

crewel. A hand-embroidery technique from Kashmir in which fine, loosely twisted two-ply yarn is chain-stitched on cotton. 99, 99

crimping. A process in which natural or synthetic fibers are set in wavy coils for resilience, wrinkle resistance, and natural cohesion in finishing. 50, 54, 56, 57, 64

crochet. A single-element construction made by interlooping stitches with a hooked needle. 70, 75

crocking. The rubbing off of excess dyestuff from dry or wet fabric. 34, 109, 120, 121

cross dyeing. Piece-dyeing fabric that incorporates two generically different fibers with two different dyestuffs to produce checks, stripes, or other combinations characteristic of yarn-dyed goods. 108

crushed fabrics. Pile fabrics, such as crushed velvet, crushed velour, and plush, which are treated with heat, moisture, and pressure in finishing to distort the pile formation. 90

Cumuloft. Trade name of a texturized nylon produced by Monsanto. 56, 58

cuprammonium rayon. A type of rayon made from cellulose dissolved in an ammoniacal copper solution. 57

custom services. 57, 58

cut. The cutting module or unfinished panel length of a window or wall fabric. 123

cut order. A fabric ordered to a specific measurement, as opposed to piece-goods business. 129

cut pile. A fabric or carpet in which the pile is cut rather than looped. 36, 76, 100, 105

cut wire. A rod tipped with a sharp blade, which forms a loop, then cuts it to make cut-pile fabrics. 90

cutwork. Continuous brocading in which floats of a supplementary weft are cut off to expose a sheer ground. 88

Dacron. Trade name of a polyester fiber made by Du Pont. 59

damask. A woven pattern based upon contrasting warp-face and filling-face cloths. 17, 46, 77, 82, 82, 84, 85

decatizing. A basic finishing process that amounts to light scouring and single calendering. 97

deep-dye fibers. Modified fibers that result in darker, tone-on-tone effects when dyed together with normal fibers of the same type. 57, 108

degumming. The process of boiling off the natural gums from silk yarn or fabric. 55

delustring. A chemical process in which the luster of man-made yarn or fabric is reduced by changing the character of its light reflection, either before spinning, by inserting colorless pigments into the solution, or during spinning, by altering the contour, cross section, or density of a filament.

demi-line. An intermediate quality of linen. 52

denier. A unit of weight that indicates the size of a filament: the higher the denier, the heavier the yarn. 50, 58

denim. Yarn-dyed cotton cloth woven in a warp-faced twill, usually with a dyed warp and a natural filling. 77, 82

density. The measure of the set of a cloth: the total number of ends and picks. 8, 16, 21, 31, 50, 72, 82, 88, 90, 97, 105

dent. The space between the teeth in the reed on a loom, which controls the spacing of the warp ends. 16

developed dye. A dye that oxidizes and changes color after application. 109

diaper. An allover repeating pattern produced by combining herringbone weave and a reversed twill. 17, 77, 82

dimensional stability. The degree to which a fabric will retain its original shape or size. 22, 33, 50, 52, 58, 59, 68

Diolen. Trade name of a German polyester. 59

direct dyes. A class of dyes that are used for cellulosics and need no fixatives. 109

direct printing. A general term for a printing process in which color is applied directly onto the fabric. 115

discharge printing. A printing process in which the pattern is bleached out of already dyed goods; it may be replaced with another color. 115

discontinuous brocade. A fabric in which small areas of weft are woven back and forth to complete a pattern. 76, 88, *89*

disperse dyeing. A dyeing process for acetate, acrylic, nylon, and polyester in which a dye only slightly water-soluble is dispersed in the fiber solution. Without proper precautions the dye is subject to fume fading and sublimation. 108, 109, 115

dobby. An attachment for a multiple-harness loom that produces simple **dobby patterns,** such as bird's-eye. 17, 79, 90, 92

Dolan. Trade name for an acrylic fiber made by Hoechst.

dope dyeing. Trade jargon for solution dyeing. 59

dotted swiss. A sheer cloth with a spaced pattern, produced by dense areas of supplementary filling in a swivel weave. The dots may be clipped. 76, 88, *89*

double cloth. A compound cloth based on two sets each of warp and filling held together at regular intervals by a warp or filling thread passing from one fabric to the other. 17, *31*, 47, 76, 77, 92, 93, 105

double-faced fabric. A reversible fabric, usually with one set of warp yarns and two sets of filling yarns, one on each face.

double knit. A knitted fabric made with a double set of needles to produce a double thickness of fabric, which is denser and has more dimensional stability than a single knit; it is sometimes double-faced as well. 34, 76, 94

douppioni. A silk yarn reeled from two cocoons that have grown together, resulting in a slubby, interrupted texture. 55

downtown house. A fabric house that sells to retailers and uptown and regional houses. 130

Dralon. Trade name of a German acrylic made by Bayer. 59

draw. (1) To shape or stretch out a fiber or yarn. (2) In weaving, to move warp threads through the heddles in the proper order to produce a pattern. 60

drill. A strong cloth, originally cotton, of twill construction. 77

drip-dry. A cloth that can be hung to dry without spinning or wringing and thus needs no ironing. This characteristic may be inherent in a fabric or induced by special finishes. 58

dry cleaning. See cleaning.

dry spinning. (1) Spinning fiber, particularly linen, when dry to produce a lofty, soft yarn. (2) See spinning (2). 52

duck. A lightweight, plain-woven cotton canvas. 72, 76

durable press. See permanent press.

duvetyn. A cotton cloth with a velvety nap that covers the entire surface.

dye, or **dyestuff.** Soluble color matter, either natural or manufactured, that will fuse with fiber molecules under certain conditions. 33, 35, 104, 105, 106, 107, 108

dye affinity. The susceptibility of a fiber to attract and fix various dyestuffs. 54, 108, 111, 115

dyeing. Classes of 108; direct 109; fiber-reactive 109; piece 105; procion 109; solution 104; stock 105; union 108; vat 109; yarn 105

Dynel. Trade name of a modacrylic fiber produced by Union Carbide. 59

Egyptian cotton. An extra-long-staple cotton from Egypt. 50, *80*

eiderdown. A felted-wool roving. 61, 62

electric pistol. A hand-guided single-needle machine used to tuft yarn into a pattern drawn on a canvas backing. 100

electrostatic flocking. A process in which short, chopped fibers are electrically charged to adhere to an adhesive-coated cloth.

The fibers stand bolt upright to provide a velvetlike pile. 115

element. A single yarn or set of yarns that behaves in like manner in the construction of a fabric. 46, 47, 68, *70*, 71, 88, 92, 93

elongation. The stretch of a fiber, yarn, or fabric. 50, 121

embossing. A decorative fabric finish produced by patterned rollers. 34, 64, 69, 97

embroidery. A basic cloth embellished by ornamental needlework. 17, 43, 99, 100

end. An individual warp yarn. 32, 47, 72, 90, 97, 122

end-and-end cloth. A plain-woven cloth, originally cotton, in which textural pattern is produced by alternating ends of dark and light yarns.

Enjay. Trade name of a saran (monofilament or slit film only) produced by Eastman. 59

Enkaloft. Trade name of a high-bulk texturized nylon produced by American Enka.

Enkalure. Trade name of a multilobal nylon produced by American Enka.

Enkrome. Trade name of an acid-dyeable rayon produced by American Enka. 58

Enkron. Trade name of a polyester fiber produced by American Enka.

Estron. Trade name of an acetate produced by Eastman. 58

etch printing. See burn-out printing.

Everglaze. Trade name of a relatively permanent chintzing process patented by Joseph Bancroft. 97

extruded fabric. A nonfibrous fabric, related to film, that is made directly from a solution. *70*, 70, 74

fabric. The most general textile term, embracing the gamut of cloths, rugs, carpets, tapestries, mattings, canings, etc. Choice and specification 22, 36, 43; cleaning and spotting 35; construction 68; direction 36; functions of 20 (window), 28 (furniture), 36 (walls and ceilings), performance 22; physical properties of 8 (texture), 12 (color), 15 (pattern)

fabric house. 130

fabric industry. 128

face. The side on which a fabric is finished. 36, 82, 90, 93

Fade-Ometer. A machine that uses a carbon-arc ultraviolet light to test the relative resistance of fabrics or yarns to color loss in sunlight. 121

fading. Color fugitive to light, pollutants, cleaning, etc. 121

faille. A lightweight fabric, originally silk, with a pronounced transverse rib. 79

fall-on. See overlay.

fancy twill. A twill that requires eight or more harnesses to weave. 82

fault. An eccentric characteristic, usually of an entire piece or lot of fabric. 33, 52, 91, 108, 122, 123

felt. (1) A fabric made from fibers not taken to yarn form but instead intermeshed by heat, moisture, and agitation. (2) A supported felt, formed over a meshlike armature to obtain additional strength. (3) A fabric made by shrinking and agitating woven or knit cloth to obtain superior density, resilience, and strength. 36, 46, 47, 54, 68, 75, 97

fiber. To qualify as a textile fiber, a substance must possess a high length-to-breadth ratio; adequate strength; flexibility, or pliability; cohesiveness, or good spinning quality; and uniformity. Cellulosic 25, 58; classification 50; mineral 58; natural 50; protein 53; qualities and properties 48, 51, 52, 54, 55; strength 58, 59; synthetic 57; terms 49; trade names 58, 59

Fiberglas. Trade name of a glass fiber produced by Owens-Corning. 58

fiberglass. A man-made mineral fiber extruded in continuous filaments. 22, 24, 57, 108, 109

Fibro. Trade name of a spun-viscose yarn produced by Cortaulds. 58

filament. A continuous strand of silk or man-made fiber, usually also available in cut-filament, or staple, form. The diametric size of a filament is measured in deniers. 24, 34, 47, 49, 50, 55, 56, 57, 60, 64, 68, 84, 95

filet lace. A handmade lace with a knotted, netlike foundation. The pattern is formed by filling in squares of the mesh. 75

filling, **weft**, or **woof**. An element carried horizontally on a shuttle through the open shed of the vertical warp in a woven fabric. 13, 33, 41, 47, 71, 79, 81, 84, 88, 90, 92, 95, 113, 115, 124

film. A nonfibrous, no-element fabric primarily used as a substrate or laminate. 22, 46, 47, 57, 60, 62, 68, 69, *69*, 70, 75

finishes. A term covering a broad spectrum of conversion processes. Some are **standard**, routinely done before a fabric is marketed; others serve a particular **function**, such as water repellence; still others are **special**, such as chintzing, and change the appearance of a fabric. Antibacterial, or antiseptic 98; antistatic 98; chemical 97; custom 124; faults and flaws 122; flame-retardant 98; functional 97; mothproof 97; permanent-press 98; soil-repellent 98; special 97; standard 96; wrinkle-resistant 97

Finn weave. A hand-woven double cloth with complex, often pictorial motifs. 76

fishnet. A diagonally knotted fabric sometimes used for casements. 75

flame inhibitor. A functional finish, often applied in conjunction with other finishes and sold under a variety of trade names.

flame-resistant fabric. A fabric whose fiber content or topical finish makes it difficult to ignite and slow to burn. 25, 26, 57, 58, 121

flame-retardant fabric. A man-made fabric whose fiber content is officially acceptable for most situations. 25, 40, 96, 120, 121, 125

flammable or **inflammable**. Easily set on fire. 25

flannel. A woolen fabric whose surface is slightly napped in finish. 54, 96, 97

flat-bed knit. A single-element weft-knitted fabric.

flaw. An inconsistency within a cloth. 64, 75, 122

flax. (1) The plant from the stem of which bast fiber is extracted by retting to produce linen. (2) an erroneous term for linen fiber, particularly in blends. 51, 52

fleece. (1) The woolly coat of a sheep, usually clipped in one large piece. (2) A deep, soft, woolly pile fabric. 53, 54, 97

float. The portion of a warp or filling yarn that rides over two or more opposing yarns to form a sleek face, as in satin, or is grouped to form a pattern on the face, as in brocade. 32, 36, 75, 81, 82, 84, 85, 88, 122

flocked fabric. A fabric in which the entire surface is covered with flocking to produce a velvetlike or suedelike texture. 90

flocking. A process by which a velvety pilelike surface is formed by securing short fiber ends to a fabric with adhesive. 90

flock printing. A screen- or roller-printing process in which areas are flocked to produce a patterned fabric. 115

floss. A strand made up of multiple plies with only a slight twist to give maximum coverage. 61, 62

fly. The contamination of a yarn or fabric by a foreign bit of color or fiber during spinning or weaving. 122

fly-shuttle loom. A hand loom in which the shuttle is shot through the warp shed by pulling a cord. 7

foam. A man-made no-element fabric primarily used as a substrate or backing for another fabric. 31, 34, 35, 39, 40, 43, 47, 69, 70, 75, 101

fold dyeing. A form of tie-dyeing in which the cloth is first pleated, then wrapped very tightly to resist dye penetration. 112, *125*

Fortisan. Trade name for a filament rayon produced by Celanese.

Fortrel. Trade name for a polyester fiber produced by Fiber Industries (a division of Celanese). 59

frieze. A warp-pile fabric with uncut loops. 76, 90, 91

fulling. A finishing operation, dependent on the felting property of wool, that shrinks the fabric to make it heavier and thicker. 97

fume fading. See atmospheric fading.

functional finishes. Finishes that improve the performance of a fabric. 97

fusing. A process in which thermoplastic fibers or yarns are melted together, as in ribbons, or heat-sealed, as in joinings, to form a fused edge.

fuzzing. A gradual raising of fiber ends due to wear on the fabric surface, forming patches of matted fibers which retain soil and are unsightly in appearance. 32, 120

gabardine. A worsted cloth characterized by a sharp diagonal twill and a polished surface. 50, 54, 76

gas fading. See atmospheric fading.

gauze. An openly constructed, transparent cloth of any fiber. 76, 88

gauze weave. A lenolike construction in which pairs or other groupings of warp ends are twisted between insertions of weft.

generic fibers. Universally accepted classifications of chemically distinct families of fibers. 49, 57, 108

gimp. A silk or metallic yarn spiral-wrapped closely around an inner core to cover it completely. 61, *63*, 64, 81

gingham. A yarn-dyed, combed or carded cotton fabric woven into a series of simple patterns in two or more colors, such as checks, stripes, and plaids. 76, 79

glazing. A general term for a polished finish on a cloth, often using waxes or resins and hot rollers. 46, 96, 97

goat hair. (1) Common coarse, scratchy hair used for tribal rugs. (2) Cashmere. (3) Mohair. 54, 55

Göbelin. Tapestry made at the Göbelin works near Paris. 76

goose-eye. See bird's-eye.

grain. The alignment of vertical and horizontal elements in a fabric, approaching a right-angle relationship. 43

grass cloth. A wall covering of honeysuckle-bark fibers woven across a spaced cotton warp, then laminated onto paper.

grass fibers. A general class of fibers that includes abaca, lauhala, sea grass, grain straw, bamboo, rattan, and cane. 53, 60, 104

gray goods, or **greige**. Raw or unfinished goods that have been woven but not finished or converted. 51, 52, 104, 128, 129

grin. A small area of ground color that shows through if the print is off-register. 112

grosgrain. (1) A heavy, corded ribbon or cloth. (2) A large-scale frieze cloth with a heavy, regular warp pile. 76, 79

grospoint. An upholstery fabric with an uncut looped pile.

grouping. Carrying two or more yarns as one. 76, 90

hair fibers. Animal fibers that lack the crimp and resilience of wool, cashmere, or camel's hair, such as common goat hair, rabbit hair, and fur fibers. 54, 55

halftone. A subtle shading from one color to another. 111, 114, 115, 116

halo. A partially dyed area around the pattern of a discharge print. 39, 115

hand. Literally, the feel of the goods in the hand, a qualitative term used to describe the tactile properties of a fabric. 34, 51, 64, 97, 108

handkerchief linen. A sheer, plain-woven linen sometimes used for curtains.

hand-loomed. Woven on a fly-shuttle hand loom. 71

hand-printing processes. A variety of preindustrial printing techniques that are done by hand, including resist, block, and screen prints. 114

hand-spun yarns. *62*, 64, *64*, 109, 123

hand tests for fiber identification. 120

hang test. A means of checking the degree of shrinkage or stretch of a window fabric by hanging a length of it in climatic conditions similar to those in the permanent location. 121

hank. See skein.

hank, or **skein**, **dyeing**. Dyeing loose skeins of yarn in a large vat in which skeins, liquid, or both are in motion. 105

harness. The part of the loom containing the heddles through which warp yarns are threaded. 71, *71*, 82

heather mixture. A yarn composed of a mixture of fibers dyed in different colors. *62*, 105, 108

heat sensitivity. A characteristic of protein and thermoplastic synthetic fibers, which results in shrinkage, discoloration, and/or deterioration. 59

heat setting. A process in which fabrics of thermoplastic fibers are tentered under controlled heat to stabilize dimensions and to minimize future shrinkage or stretching. 22, 49, 64, 94, 96, 98

heat-transfer printing. See transfer printing.

heddle. One of the sets of parallel cords or wires that compose the harness and control individual warp ends. 71, *71*

Helanca. Trade name of a stretch-nylon process developed by Heberlein.

hemp. A high-strength bast fiber. 52, *65*, 92, 120

henequen. A coarse, hard fiber that resembles sisal.

Herculon. Trade name of a polypropylene fiber produced by Hercules. 59

herringbone. A twill weave that reverse direction across the fabric to form a chevron. *31*, 82, *83*

high tenacity. Unusual strength, a characteristic of several man-made fibers modified for specific end uses. 57

high wet modulus rayon. A modified rayon with greater dimensional stability in washing. 57, 58

hiking, or **yoyo.** The alternate sagging and shrinking of casement panels due to humidity changes. 22, 24

hole. A fabric defect that results from either the beater crashing down on a shuttle trapped in the warp or a broken end in a warp knit. 122

homespun. A slubby single-ply yarn with some of the random character of hand-spun yarn. 54, 99

honan. A lustrous tussah silk, originally hand-woven in the Honan province of China. 55

honeycomb. A hexagonally patterned piqué weave. *81*

hopsacking. A coarse, loose, plain- or basket-woven fabric of cotton or other yarns. 76

horizontal operation. A business involved with a single aspect of fabric production, which it sells to a varied market. 128

horsehair. A narrow upholstery fabric woven with a filling of long, single-tail hair. 32, 36, 49, 55, 60

houndstooth. A four-pointed twill-woven check.

huckaback. A dobby weave originally used in cotton or linen toweling. 17, 81

hydrophilic. Moisture-absorbent. 24, 43, 50, 98, 105

hydrophobic. Moisture-repellent. 22, 24, 25, 35, 50, 109

ikat. A fabric woven with tie-dyed yarns. 112, *125*

interlining. A layer of fabric between the outer, decorative fabric and the lining. 21

intimate blend. A blend of two or more compatible fibers that are carded together so that no one characteristic dominates. 108

jacquard. A pattern-controlling attachment for looms and knitting and lace machines. 17, 73, 76, 82, 92, 93

jaspé. A fabric with a progression of light, medium, and dark shades of the same color.

jersey. A tubular fabric knitted on a circular machine. 70, 94

Jetspun. Trade name for a solution-dyed rayon yarn produced by American Enka. 58

jig dyeing. A form of piece dyeing in which an open width of cloth is repeatedly run through a stationary dyebath. 108

jobber. A mercantile company that buys large lots of fabric from a producer or converter and wholesales in smaller quantities. 129, 130

jute. A long bast fiber from the stalk of an Indian plant. 51, 52, 104

Kanekalon. A Japanese modacrylic fiber produced by Kanekafuchi. 59

kenaf. A bast fiber similar to jute.

kid mohair. The finest mohair, produced from the first shearing of the Angora goat. 54

kilim. A pileless tapestry-woven carpet, mat, or spread. 76, 79

kiss coat. A very light fabric backing. 100

knitting. A single-element fabric construction formed by interlacing yarn or thread in a series of connected loops with needles. 46

knot. A flaw found in yarn joinings. 61, 63, *64*, 122

knotting. Fancywork produced by twisting and looping threads into knots to form designs. 25

Kodel. Trade name of a polyester staple fiber produced by Eastman. 59

Konol. The trade name of a novolid fiber produced by Union Carbide. 57

lace. An openly constructed, patterned cloth. 68, 70, 76, 93, 94

laminated fabric. Fabric created by bonding two or more layers of material together. 39, 40, 69, 75, 100

lappet. A three-element woven fabric similar to discontinuous brocade. 76, 88

lauhala. A grass fiber that is plaited on the diagonal for coarse matting. 53

laundering. Cleaning a fabric by immersion in a soap-and-water solution. 24, 90, 94, 104; Preshrinking 24; shampoiing 24, 97

Leacril. Trade name for an Italian acrylic fiber produced by Montedison. 59

leno, or **marquisette.** A woven fabric construction in which two or more warp ends twist between insertions of weft. 25, 79, *80*, *81*, *88*

lightfastness. Color resistance to light. 58, 59

line linen. Selected long linen fibers with superior strength and luster. 52

linen. A fiber extracted from the flax plant. 24, 25, 33, 50, 51, 79, 90, 96, 97, 98, 100, 104, 108, 120

linen system. A spinning process, originally developed for linen, in which long fibers are combed, plied, and spun. 60

lining. Material attached under the principal material of a cloth or article. 22, 24, 41, 132

llama. A South American camelidae whose fleece grows in a variety of natural colors and is similar to but coarser than alpaca. 55

loft. Permanent high bulk. 50, 54

loom. A frame or machine for interlacing at right angles two or more sets of threads or yarns to form a cloth. 46, 64, 70, 71, 72, 96, 122, 129

loom-state. Goods as they come off the loom before they are finished or converted. 97, 123

Lurex. Trade name of a slit-film metallic yarn produced by Dow Badische. 60, 75

luster. The gloss or sheen on the surface of a fabric or yarn. 8, 50, 54, 55, 57, 62, 97, *105*

Lycra. Trade name of a spandex fiber produced by Du Pont. 64

macramé. A coarse single-element construction employing a variety of knots in a geometrical pattern. 75

madagascar. A hand-woven cloth of palm fiber, known as raffia. 53

Malimo. A nonwoven multiple-element fabric construction in which hundreds of stitching yarns knit the weft onto the warp. 76, 93, *95*

Manila hemp. See abaca.

man-made fibers. An inclusive term for all manufactured fibers. 12, 13, 24, 26, 34, 35, 48, 49, 50, 53, 56, 57, 58, 60, 68, 104

marled yarn. A yarn in which two or more plies of different colors or textures are twisted together. 61

marquisette. (1) See leno. (2) A leno-woven sheer of cotton or synthetic yarn used for glass curtains. 76

Martindale test. A European test for abrasion resistance. 121

match. The relative constancy of shade from one dye lot to another. 110. Pattern match 36, 40, 132

matelassé. A jacquard-woven double cloth in which the pattern repeat resembles a quilted surface. 10, 17, 75, 76, 92

melton. A heavy, felted, dark-colored cloth, often of reprocessed wool. 54, 97

melt spinning. See spinning (2).

mercerizing. A caustic-soda treatment for cotton and linen, which makes the yarn or cloth stronger and increases luster and dye affinity. 50, 52, 96, 112

merino. A fine wool with high crimp from the merino sheep. 50, 54

metallic. A general term for a manufactured fiber composed of metal, plastic-coated metal, or a core completely covered by metal. 9, 26, 57, 61, *63*, 69, 75, 81, 109

metamerism. A term for colors that match under some but not all light sources. 110

Metlon. Trade name of an aluminum metallic yarn produced by Metlon.

Milium. Trade name of an aluminum-powder backing produced by Deering Milliken, which is applied to window fabric to reflect heat.

mineral fiber. A general term for natural and man-made fibers derived from minerals, such as asbestos and fiberglass. 24

Minicare. Trade name for a resin finish that eliminates wrinkles and ironing produced by Joseph Bancroft.

mispick. A horizontal or vertical float caused by a filling yarn that does not engage warp ends properly. 122

Mitin. Trade name of a permanent mothproofing process for wools and wool blends produced by Geigy.

mock leno. A lacy woven construction. 75

modacrylic. A generic term for a modified-acrylic fiber composed of copolymers of acrylonitrile and other materials such as vinyl chloride, which enable the fiber to be softened at low temperatures. 26, 59, 109

mohair. The extremely long, silky fiber from the Angora goat. 9, 26, 54, 62, 63, 90, 97, 108

moiré. A wavy, watered pattern. 97

monk's cloth. A basket-woven cotton fabric. 72, 76

monofilament. A yarn composed of a single untwisted and un-plied synthetic filament. 9, 32, *49*, 56, 60, *62*, 95

mordant. A metallic salt used to fix dyes. 108, 109

moresque. A yarn with plies of two or more colors used to produce a random pattern, especially in carpets and pile fabrics. 61

motif. A pattern unit, usually repeated. 15

Moygashel. Trade name of fine Irish linen cloths produced by Moygashel.

muga silk. A spun wild silk with a lustrous surface, creamy hand, and ivory color.

multifilament. A yarn composed of several extruded filaments. 56, 60, *61*, 62, 64

muslin. A plain-woven, uncombed-cotton fabric, ranging from sheer to coarse in texture. 34, 72, 76, 79

Mylar. Trade name for a polyester available as a clear film or as a laminate produced by Du Pont. 60, 75 *100*

nap. A hairy or downy surface.

naphthol dye. A developed dye that produces brilliant reds and oranges in cellulosic fabrics. 109

napping. A finishing process in which circular brushes vigorously raise the fiber ends, forming a pilelike surface. 36, 90, 97

natural fibers. A general term for fibers derived from natural substances such as cellulose, proteins, and minerals. 48, 50, 57, 60, 104

Naugahyde. Trade name of a vinyl fabric produced by UniRoyal. 30, 75, 101

needle punching. A form of no-element structuring in which webs of fibers are laid down in various ways and stitched together by hundreds of barbed needles, which push the fibers through the web in a disordered, entangled arrangement. The thickness of the web determines its end use—from light open-work effects to a dense mesh used for carpets. 68, 69, 75

net. (1) A general term for a lacy diamond-shaped mesh. (2) A coarse open-meshed fabric made by diagonal square knotting, such as fishnet. 75

ninon. A smooth, sheer, plain-woven fabric for casements.

no-element fabrics. Fabrics which are either fibrous but not taken to yarn form or nonfibrous—made directly from a solution. 68, 69, 75

noil. (1) Textile fiber too short to be spun. (2) Short-fiber or

waste silk spun on the cotton system; it has a dull surface but retains the airy fall of silk fabric. 54, 55

Nomex. Trade name for a flame-retardant and heat-resistant aramid fiber produced by Du Pont. 26, 57, 58

nonwoven fabrics. No-element fabrics made from fibers not taken to yarn form. 47, 54, 68, *69*, 75, 76

nottingham lace. A machine-made flat lace or net. 17, *18*, 25, 94, *95*

novelty yarns. Yarns in which a fine base or core yarn is loosely wrapped with a bulkier effect yarn and secured with a tie yarn. 61

novolid. A generic term for a new type of man-made fiber with inherently high flame resistance. 57

nub. A random clot of short, dense fibers incorporated during spinning. 61, 112

nylon. A generic term for the synthetic polyamide fibers. 24, 26, 32, 46, 48, 49, 58, 97, 98, 108, 109, 114

nytril. A generic term for a synthetic fiber composed largely of vinylidene dinitrile.

off-grain. A finishing fault in which the horizontal structure runs on a diagonal. 123

oilcloth. A cotton cloth coated with a dull or glossy oil finish to make it waterproof.

olefin. A generic term for synthetic fibers produced from either polyethylene or polypropylene. 26, 35, 59

ombré. Color graduated from light to dark. 13

on-grain. True right-angle alignment of vertical and horizontal elements, necessary in fabrics with a strong horizontal emphasis for matching, printed patterns, or proper draping. 43

organdy. A sheer, plain-woven cotton cloth with a crisp hand. 114

organza. A sheer fabric similar to organdy but made of silk, rayon, or nylon.

organzine. A fine silk yarn, consisting of two or three filaments twisted together, that is used for warp threads.

Orlon. Trade name of an acrylic fiber produced by Du Pont. 59

osnaburg. A rough, unbleached, plain-woven cotton characterized by dark boll particles.

ottoman. A heavy horizontal-ribbed fabric, usually with a densely set warp of silk, acetate, or rayon and a cotton or wool weft. 79

outline quilting. A form of quilting in which the stitching follows the motif of a printed fabric. 101

overdyeing. A form of piece dyeing in which a partly dyed cloth is dyed again, retaining the original pattern. 108

overlay, or **fall-on.** A double-printing process in which overlapping color areas become darker or of a different hue. 111

overshot. A weft brocade. 88

Ozite. Trade name of a felted fabric of coarse animal hair produced by Ozite, generally used as an underlay for carpets. 75

package dyeing. A form of yarn dyeing in which the dye liquid and the rinse bath are forced through a large number of one-pound packages of yarn. 105

pad dyeing. A method of dyeing in which color is applied to fabric by cloth-covered rollers. 103, 108, 109

palm fibers. A general class of fibers obtained from palm trees, shrubs, or vines, such as madagascar. 53

panné. A mechanical finish for velvets and velours in which heat and pressure lay the pile on a steep diagonal, thus increasing pile cover and luster. 90

paper yarn. A natural, bleached, or dyed yarn produced from twisted paper. 60

passementerie. A fancy edging or trimming made of braid, cord, gimp, beading, or metallic thread.

pattern. A structural or applied configuration that forms a unit of design. 15, 72, 90

pattern repeat. A total design unit. 15, 97, 112

Pellon. Trade name of a nonwoven backing or interlining produced by Pellon. 75

penetration. The depth to which a yarn or fabric absorbs a dyestuff. 112

percale. A fine, plain-woven cloth of closely set combed and carded long-staple cotton.

Perlon. Trade name of a German nylon fiber produced by Bayer. 57

permanent, or **durable, press.** A finish applied to fabric by means of resins in solution or gaseous form and cured under conditions of controlled heat to set the shape and to make it wrinkle-resistant in machine washing. 98

pick. An individual shot of filling yarn, often taken as a unit of the fineness of the cloth. 71, 84, 122

piece dyeing. The dyeing of cloth after production, as opposed to dyeing fibers or yarns before production. 105, 108

pigment. An insoluble powdered coloring agent carried in a liquid binder and printed or padded onto the surface of a cloth. 33, 90, 103, 104, 105, 108, 109, 112, 124, 129

pile. A velvety surface produced by an extra set of filling yarns that form raised loops, which may be cut and sheared or left uncut. 10, 47, 90, 93, 97, 120

pile weave. A fabric with cut or uncut loops above the surface of the ground cloth, such as terrycloth and velvet. 47, 76, *91*

pill. A fuzzy ball caused by the rolling up of abraded surface fibers. 32, 56, 58, 59, 120

pillow. A lightly stuffed cushion used to support the design in making bobbin lace.

pilot plant. A small mill or mill unit dealing only with fabric development.

pima cotton. An extra-long-staple fiber with a silky sheen and exceptional strength and firmness, developed in the American Southwest by selective cross-breeding of Egyptian and American cottons. 48

piña. A crisp, grassy fiber from the leaves of the pineapple plant. 51, 53

piqué. A durable fabric, either ribbed or in a honeycomb or waffle weave. 8, 75

plaid. A pattern of unevenly spaced repeated stripes crossing at right angles. 16

plain weave. The simplest and most basic woven construction, in which one end interlaces alternately with one pick. 10, 36, 47, 72, *74*, 75, 76, *78*, *80*, 81, 82, 85, *92*, *105*, 122

plissé. A puckered or blistered design effect formed by shrinking fabric in selected areas with a caustic soda solution (cotton) or with heat (synthetics). 115

plush. A pile-woven cloth with a higher and less dense pile than velvet or velour. 38, 72, 76, 90, 93

ply. (1) A single strand of yarn. (2) To twist two or more strands of yarn together. 32, 57, 61, 64

pocket weave. A double cloth in which the two cloth layers are joined only at the pattern change. 92

polished cotton. A combed and carded fabric, usually of twill or satin construction, which is calendered to produce a high luster. 97

polyester. A generic term for a manufactured fiber in which the fiber-forming substance is a long-chain synthetic polymer composed of a complex ester. 22, 24, 49, 59, 62, 69, 94, 98, 101, 108, 109, 114, 115, *116*

polymer. A chemical compound consisting of repeating structural units, the basis of most synthetic fibers. 57

pongee. A plain-woven raw-silk fabric with an ecru-heather effect caused by natural color variation within the fibers. 55

poplin. A plain-woven, warp-faced fabric with a fine crosswise rib running from selvage to selvage. 79

porosity. The ease with which air and water can pass through a cloth. 31

PPG. Trade name of a glass fiber produced by Pittsburgh Plate Glass. 58

preshrinking. The shrinking of a fabric during manufacture, usually to reduce later shrinking in laudering. 22, 35, 90, 94, 96, 97

printcloth. A basic fabric produced in quantity for printing.

printing. The process of impressing a pattern or design on cloth. 69, 103, 111, 129; Automatic or machine-screen 114; batik 112; block 113; burn-out 115; discharge 115; flock 115;

fold dyes 112; reserve or resist 115; roller 114; screen 114; tie-dyes 112; transfer 115

procion dye. A fiber-reactive dye that produces bright shades with excellent fastness and washability. 109

progressive shrinkage. Continued shrinking resulting from exposure to extremes of heat or humidity or from successive cleaning procedures.

protein fibers. A general term for natural fibers derived from animal protein, such as wool, silk, and hair; animal protein is also used for various man-made fibers produced from casein bases. 25, 46, 53, 54, 55, 97, 108, 109

polyvinyl chloride (PVC), or **vinyon.** A generic term for a synthetic fiber composed primarily of vinyl chloride. 26, 69

Qiana. Trade name of a luxurious silklike nylon produced by Du Pont. 58

quilting. The stitching together of two or more layers of fabric, generally separated by one or more layers of fiber batting. 76, 93, 101, 125; Outline 101; trapunto 101; vermicelli 101

Rachel knit. A fabric woven on a Rachel warp-knitting machine. 76, 94, *94*

raffia. See magadascar.

railroad. To run a vertically striped pattern horizontally 36, 84

ramie. A fine oriental bast fiber. 51, 52

ratiné. A novelty yarn with one heavy ply twisted back and forth across a threadlike core. 61, 63

rattan. A palm fiber often used for wickerwork. 53

raveling. The fraying of yarns out of cut ends of cloth. 40, 97, 120

raw silk. Silk that is not fully degummed; it is stiff, tacky, and naturally caramel in color. 55

rayon. Generic term for a man-made fiber derived from regenerated cellulose. 24, 25, 49, 57, 63, 68, 96, 105, 108, 115

reactive dyes. A class of dyes that react chemically with fiber molecules and produce fast, bright colors. 109

recovery. The ability of a stretch yarn or cloth to return to its original shape or size. 34, 64, 120

reed, or **comb.** The comblike device in the beater of a loom that spaces the warp ends and beats in the filling picks. 71, 122

reed mark. A vertical streak in woven fabric caused by a bent wire in the reed. 122

reeled silk. Continuous filament silk as it is reeled off the softened cocoon of the cultivated silkworm. 55

regenerated cellulose. Cellulosic material derived from cotton linters or wood pulp and dissolved, purified, and extruded to form rayon, acetate, and triacetate. 57, 58

registration. The alignment of print screens or rollers to make a precise pattern. 112, 114

remnant. A small piece of cloth, usually less than three yards.

rep. A plain-woven fabric characterized by raised, rounded ribs running from selvage to selvage.

reprocessed fiber. Fiber obtained from scraps of unused fabric, which are shredded into a fibrous state and carded and spun like ordinary fiber. 54, 78

reserve printing. See resist printing.

residual shrinkage. Shrinkage occurring during use and cleaning, following the relaxation shrinkage of finishing processes.

resilience. The stretch and return of a fiber, yarn, or fabric. 32, 33, 40, 52, 54, 56, 57, 58, 59, 70

resin. A synthetic substance used in corrective finishes to add body, reduce creasing, control shrinkage, produce luster in glazing, repel water, or supply permanent press. 97, 98, 109, 120

resist, or **reserve, printing.** A general term for printing processes in which the motif or the ground is treated with a dye-resistant substance before dyeing the fabric. 112, 113, 115

retting. The soaking of bast plants to permit bacterial or chemical breakdown of the outer bark, which loosens the fibers. 51

reused fiber. Fiber recycled from rags and waste, usually mixed or blended with other fibers. 54

reverse twill weave. A patterned twill weave utilizing both right- and left-hand progressions. 77, 82, *82*

Rhonel. Trade name of a French triacetate produced by Rhône-Poulenc. 58

Rhovyl. Trade name of a French polyvinyl-chloride fiber produced by Rhône-Poulenc.

rib weave. (1) A modification of plain weave in which fine warp ends are closely set and two picks (or one heavier pick) interlace as one. (2) Any woven fabric construction with a horizontal rib or cord. 74, 76, 78

roller printing. The mechanical printing of fabric with engraved rollers. 111, 112, *114*

rotary-screen printing. A fast and accurate printing process in which the cloth moves under a series of large, patterned cylinders. 114

roving. A spun yarn before it is drawn and twisted. 52, 60, 61, 62

rubber. A generic germ for fibers composed of natural or synthetic rubber. 57

sagging. Elongation, common to many fabrics and dependent on fiber content and cloth structure. 24, 33, 35, 43

sailcloth. Lightweight, plain-woven cotton duck. 72, 76, 131

Sanforizing. Trade name of preshrinking process for cotton and linen fabrics produced by Cluett, Peabody.

saponified rayon. A rayon filament created by reconverting cellulose acetate to cellulose. 57

saran. A generic term for a man-made fiber composed of at least 80 percent polymerized vinylidene chloride. 26, 59, *94*

sateen. A filling-face satin weave used primarily for cotton drapery lining and antique satin. 76, 84, 85

satin. A warp-faced woven construction in which the yarns are interlaced at widely spaced regular or irregular intervals to form a smooth, compact, unbroken surface. 8, *15*, 30, 36, 46, 72, 76, 77, 79, 81, 84, *84*, 85, 92, *105*

schiffli embroidery. Machine-made embroidery in which the decorative yarns are held in place by a binder thread on the reverse side of the cloth. 17, 100, *100*

schiffli lace. A fabric produced by embroidering on a silk gauze, which is then burned away to create open areas. 100

Scotchgard. Trade name of a fluorochemical stain- and water-repellent finish produced by Minnesota Mining and Manufacturing. 35, 98

scouring. A finishing process in which warm or hot water is combined with soap or detergent to full the cloth and remove grease. 64, 96, 105, 112, 123

screen printing. A hand- or machine-printing process in which a pattern-making stencil or screen held in a frame is positioned on the cloth, and colorant applied. 114, 125

scrim. A theatrical gauze of sheer, plain-woven linen or hemp. 68

sea grass. A grass often woven into mattings such as tatami. 53

sea island cotton. An extra-long-staple fiber grown on the sea islands off the coast of Georgia. 50

second. A fabric with too many flaws to meet a given commercial standard. 122

seed yarn. A novelty yarn with hard, seedlike nubs. 61, 63

seersucker. A plain-woven cloth, often striped, with puckered or blistered vertical rows produced by a shrinking differential in two groups of warp yarns.

selvage. The edge on either side of a woven or flat-knitted fabric, often of different threads and/or weave, so finished to prevent raveling. 71, 88, 100, 108, 110, 112, 115, 122

selvage legend. Printed copy (firm, designer, pattern, color key) sometimes found running lengthwise on the fabric edge. 112

serge. A durable, solid-color, twilled fabric with a smooth, clear face and a pronounced diagonal rib on both sides. 82

set. The density of a woven cloth, particularly of its warp ends. 8, 71

shading coefficient. The amount of heat- and light deflection achieved by a casement, an important factor in calculating a room's air-conditioning requirements. 21, 121

shantung. A dense, plain-woven silk cloth with a slightly irregular surface due to uneven, slubbed filling yarns. 55

shed. The triangular opening between the raised and lowered warp ends through which the filling yarns pass. 71

sheer. A very thin, transparent, or semiopaque fabric. 21, 27, 52

sheeting. Plain-woven cotton of various qualities, the traditional ground for chintz and a basic cloth for printing.

shot. See pick.

shrinkage. The contraction of cloth due to heat and moisture. 22, 24, 33, 35, 49, 121

shuttle. The device used in weaving to carry the weft yarns across the width of the loom. 71, 122

shuttleless loom. A fast-paced loom that disposes of bobbins, shuttles, and selvages. 71

silicone finish. An applied finish to resist soil and water-borne stains. 25, 98

silk. A natural-protein fiber produced from the cocoon of wild or cultivated silkworms. 8, 26, 30, 34, 46, 48, 49, 50, 52, 55, 97, 104, *105*, 109, 120, 123

singeing. A basic finishing process, particularly for wool fabrics, in which unwanted surface fibers are burned off by passing the cloth under gas jets. 96

single. Textile jargon for a single-ply yarn. 61, 62, *72*

sisal. A strong, coarse leaf fiber used primarily for cordage and carpeting. 51, 52, 104

sizing. (1) A starch with which the prepared warp is slashed or drenched to reduce friction and to strengthen the yarn during production; it is removed in finishing. (2) Starch applied to finished cloth to give it additional body of a temporary, nonwashable nature. 96

skein, or **hank.** A loosely coiled length of yarn or thread wound on a reel. 61, 105

skein-dyed yarn. Yarn dyed at the skein stage of production. 105

skip dent. A missed dent in the reed during warping that produces a streak when woven. 16, 80, *80*

skip pick. A missing shot of filling that extends across the cloth. 122

slack twist. A yarn with little or no twist. 60, 64

slippage. A fabric fault caused by warp and filling yarns sliding on each other. 33, 34, 79, 82, 87, 120, 123 Seam slippage 34

slit film. A ribbonlike yarn in which metallic and other films are commonly available. *22*, *49*, 57, 60, 69, *94*

slub. A heavy area in an unevenly spun yarn. 55, *61*, 62, *64*, 122

slug. A fabric flaw caused by filling yarn doubling back on itself. 122

snagging. Yarns or fibers catching or pulling out of the cloth surface. 25, 32, 55, 60

solution dyeing. A dyeing process in which color is induced in man-made fibers in a preextrusion state, resulting in a tendency to superior colorfastness. 103, 104, 105

soutache. A narrow, decorative braid with a herringbone pattern. 75

space dyeing. A dyeing technique in which parts of a long skein are dipped into different color baths. 61, 63

spandex. A generic term for synthetic elastic fibers composed of segmented polyurethane. 64

special finishes. Finishes that determine the character of a fabric, such as ciré. 97

specific gravity. The ratio of the weight of a material to the weight of an equal volume of water. 50

spinneret. A small metal apparatus with fine holes through which man-made fibers are extruded. 49, 56, *56*, 104

spinning. (1) Drawing out and twisting fiber into yarn or thread. (2) Extruding man-made filaments through a spinneret into either warm air (**dry spinning**), a chemical solution (**wet spinning**), or in a melted form that is then hardened by cooling (**melt spinning**). 8, 56, 60, 61, 64

spun-bonded. A nonwoven fabric made from thermoplastic filament that is laid up in a directionless mass and welded with heat. 68, 75

spun silk. Yarn made from short, unreelable silk filaments. 55

spun yarn. Yarn spun from staple-length fiber, either natural or cut-up synthetic multifilaments. 8, 49, 54, 58, 60, 64

squeegee. A heavy rubber blade that pushes color onto the fabric in screen printing. 114

stability. The retention of size and shape in a fabric. 22, 23

standard. The accepted master dye lot to which later dye lots are matched. 110

standard finishes. Finishes that improve the hand and/or appearance of a fabric. 96, 97, 129 Beetling 97; bleaching 51, 104, 112, 115; boiling off 96; calendering 90, 97; carbonizing 96, 123; decatizing 97; fulling 97; scouring 64, 96, 105, 112, 123

staple. A fiber of relatively short length that forms a yarn rather than a filament when spun and twisted. 48, 49, 50, 51, 52, 56, 60, 84, 105

starch. A vegetable solution applied to fabric to give it temporary body and crispness.

stock dyeing. The dyeing of staple fiber prior to spinning. 105

stretch fabrics. 34, 35, 64, 85, 94, 101

Stretch yarn. Yarn with a durable, springy elongation and return. 62, 64

striae. A series of parallel narrow bands of color, often darker than the ground color. 13, 36

strike-off. A trial for color or pattern. 111, 114, 115, 125

stripe. A narrow section of a fabric differing in color or texture from the adjoining area. 16, 36, 40, 43, 85, 115, 122

stripping. See bleaching.

s-twist, or **crossband.** The conventional clockwise direction in which yarn is twisted. 61

Sublistatic printing. See transfer printing.

substrate. A fabric underlayer, generally of synthetic foam. 25, 68, 101

suedecloth. A woven or knitted fabric with a napped surface resembling suede. 36, 97

sulphur dye. A dye that produces heavy shades of black or brown in cellulosics. 109

sun rot. Deterioration caused by sun or light. 24, 33, 52

Supima. Trade name of an extra-long-staple cotton fiber processed by Supima.

swatch. A small sample of fabric. 120

swivel. An individual motif produced by discontinuous brocading. 76, 88, *89*

Syl-mer. Trade name of a silicone finish produced by Dow Badische.

synthetic fibers. General term for man-made fibers derived from petrochemicals rather than natural substances. 32, 49, 57, 60, 120

Taber test. A test for abrasion resistance in upholstery fabrics. 32, 121

table printing. A form of screen printing in which the cloth is secured to the top of a table and the printing screens are moved down the table, pattern repeat by pattern repeat. 114

taffeta. (1) A crisp, plain-woven fabric in which the filling is heavier than the warp, producing a fine, lustrous rib. (2) Plain weave. 8, 76, 79

tapestry. (1) A hand-weaving technique in which pattern is produced by interlocking discontinuous filling yarns. (2) A jacquard-woven warp brocade in which multicolored warp ends are carried on the back of the fabric. 7, 46, 76, 79, 88, *93*

Taslan. Trade name for a process of air-bulking continuous man-made filaments produced by Du Pont.

tatami. A thick, ribbed matting woven from sea grass.

Tebelizing. Trade name for a crease-resistant finish for linen, cotton, and spun rayon produced by Tootal. 98

Teflon. Trade name for a highly heat-resistant fiber produced by Du Pont.

tender goods. Fabric with very low tensile strength, usually caused by faulty finishing. 33, 91, 98, 123

tensile strength. The ability of a cloth to withstand varying degrees of tension without rupturing, a result of the tenacity of the fiber, the spinning of the yarn, and the construction of the cloth. 24, 33, 48, 51, 54, 58, 60, 61, 121

tentering. Controlling fabric width by stretching the selvages on tenterhooks during finishing.

Tergal. Trade name of a French polyester fiber produced by Rhodiaceta. 59

Terital. Trade name of an Italian polyester fiber produced by Montedison. 59

terrycloth. An uncut warp-pile fabric, plain- or jacquard-woven, of cotton, linen, or rayon. 8, 47, 76, 95, 96

Terylene. Trade name of a British polyester fiber produced by Imperial Chemical Industries. 59

testing. Standard procedures employed to determine the specific performance characteristics of a fabric. 120, 121 Abrasion-resistance 121; bacteria- and insect-resistance 121; cleaning 121; crocking 121; fading 121; fire-retardance and flame-resistance 121; hand 120; hang 121; shading-coefficient 21, 121; tensile-strength 121; wear 121

textile. A general term for woven cloth. 17, 46

Textura. Trade name of a polyester fiber produced by Rohm and Haas. 59

texture. The visual and tactile qualities of a cloth.

textured yarn. A man-made filament yarn that has been bulked or stretched. 7, 8, *9*, *10*, *11*, 13, *28*, 35, 37

texturizing. A process by which a fiber is given a permanent curl to make it lofty, resilient, and more natural in appearance. 57

thermal insulation. Insulation employed to reduce heat transfer. 21

thermoplastic fiber. A fiber that softens or fuses with heat and hardens again when cooled. 26, 47, 50, 54, 57, 96, 97, 98

thick-and-thin yarn. A novelty yarn that is given an uneven profile in spinning. 61

thread. A strand of plied-and-twisted yarn with a smooth finish that is used in sewing and stitching. 60

throwing. The modification of filament yarns by doubling, twisting, crimping, knitting, or texturizing.

ticking. A heavy, strong, linen or cotton twill with a colored warp stripe used in upholstering and as a covering for mattresses or pillows. 131

tobacco cloth. A lightweight, unsized, loosely plainwoven cotton fabric used to cover tobacco plants; a similar cloth is used to wrap food and is known as *cheesecloth*. 8

toile. A plain, coarse, twill-woven fabric, often linen. 114

toile de Jouy. An eighteenth-century French scenic pattern printed in one color on a light cotton-, linen-, or silk-toile ground. 114

top dyeing. (1) A form of stock dyeing in which a loose rope of parallel wool fibers is dyed prior to spinning. (2) Dyeing over another color.

tow. (1) A large group of continuous filaments assembled without twisting into a loose, ropy strand for cutting into staple. (2) Short-staple or broken fiber of flax, hemp, or synthetic material used for yarn, twine, or stuffing. 52

transfer, heat-transfer, or **Sublistatic, printing.** A printing process in which a pattern is printed on waxed paper and transferred to the cloth under heat and pressure. 111, 115

trapunto. A decorative quilted design in high relief that is worked through two or more layers of cloth by outlining the design in a running stitch and padding it from the underside. 101

Travis. Trade name of a nytril fiber, presently marketed only in Europe.

Trevira. Trade name of a multilobal-polyester fiber produced by Hoechst. 59

triacetate. A generic term for a man-made fiber that is a modification of acetate containing a higher ratio of acetate to cellulose. 57, 58

tricot. A plain warp-knitted fabric with a close, inelastic vertical knit. 34, 74, 94

tubular fabric. A woven, knitted, or braided fabric made in circular, seamless form.

tuft. A bunch of soft, fluffy threads cut off short and used as ornament. 33, 46, 76, 93, 100

Tunnel test. A series of three tests that measure the flame retardance of carpeting and wall coverings. 121

tussah. A brownish silk from uncultivated oriental silkworms. 55

tweed. A woolen fabric, usually of twill weave, with mixed color effects and a rough texture that derives from the yarn rather than the construction. 10, 33, *45*, 46, 54, 61

twill. A basic weave in which the filling yarns pass over one or more and under two or more warp yarns in successive progression to create the appearance of diagonal lines. *45*, 75, 77, *78*, 79, 81, *82*, *83*, 84, 92

twining. A fabric construction in which pairs of one element twist between insertions of the other element. 76

twisting. Winding two or more strands of fiber or yarn together to make a single multiple-ply thread or yarn. 32, 60

union dyeing. A general term that refers to a dyeing process in which a solid color is obtained in a cloth made of two or more fibers with different dye affinities. 108

uptown house. A fabric house that sells cut orders to the trade. 130

v-construction. In a pile weave catching the pile loops under one shot of weft. 90

vat dyeing. A dyeing process in which alkaline-soluble dyes are oxidized to produce excellent colorfastness in cellulosic fibers. 109, 115

velour. (1) A fabric with a pile or napped surface resembling velvet. (2) A woven fabric construction characterized by the insertion of an extra warp which is looped over wires and cut. 36, 76, 90, 93

velvet. (1) A fabric with a short, soft, dense pile. (2) A woven fabric construction characterized by the insertion of an extra warp which is looped over wires and cut. 8, 30, 31, 33, 35, 36, 46, 75, 76, 90, 93, *102*, 115, *126*

velveteen. A single-woven weft-pile fabric similar to velvet. 76, 90

Verel. Trade name of a modacrylic fiber produced by Eastman. *49*, 59

vermicelli. A quilting technique that produces an overall pattern of noodlelike squiggles. 101

vertical operation. A business involved with the entire production continuum. 128

vicuña. A small, wild Andean camelidae from the undercoat of which a fine, lustrous fiber is derived. 55

vinal. A generic term for a man-made fiber composed largely of vinyl alcohol.

vinyon. See polyvinyl chloride.

virgin wool. New wool of any grade. 48, 54

viscose rayon. The most common rayon, formed by converting cellulose into a soluble form and regenerating it into rayon. 57, 58, *62*, 68, 120

voided velvet. A single-woven velvet with an intaglio pattern incised in the ground cloth. 90

voile. A soft, sheer cloth plain-woven of fine crepe-spun yarns. *116*

Vycron. Trade name of a polyester fiber produced by Beaunit. 59

waffle weave. A piqué weave with a quadrangular pattern.

wale. (1) A horizontal, vertical, or diagonal rib in a fabric. (2) The vertical rib on the face of a knitted fabric. 8, 17, *38*, 81

warp. A series of yarns extending lengthwise on a loom and running parallel to the selvage. 13, 22, 24, 33, 70, 79, 81, 84, 92, 95, 105, 113, 115, 122, 124

warp knit. (1) A fabric produced on a knitting machine in which the yarns run in a lengthwise but zigzag direction, producing excellent stability in a vertical direction. (2) A tricot knit. 22, *49*, 75, 76, 83, 94, *94*

warp laminate. A set of parallel vertical yarns adhered to paper for use as a wall covering. 39, 40, 101

warp print. A pattern printed on the warp prior to weaving, which results in an indistinct image. 115

w-construction. In a pile weave catching the pile yarns under one weft and over another and tying them down on the third to keep them from pulling out of the face of the cloth. 90

weaving. Interlacing warp and filling yarns to form a pliable fabric. 71 Brocade 88; damask 85; dobby 17; jacquard 17; pile 90; plain, or taffeta 72; sateen 85; satin 84; tapestry 79; twill 82; velour 90; velvet 90

weft. See filling.

weighted silk. Silk treated with tin salts to increase weight and apparent value, an obsolete and illegal practice. 55

welt. A fabric-covered cord inserted in the seams of upholstery and cushions for ornament or reinforcement. 32, 36, 52

wet finishes. See chemical finishes.

wet spinning. (1) Spinning fiber, particularly linen and hemp, while damp to produce a smooth, wiry yarn. (2) See spinning (2). 52, 92

wet strength. The relative resistance of a wet fiber, yarn, or fabric to tension and abrasion.

wickerwork. The interlacing of pliable osiers, twigs, or rods, often used for furniture.

wild silk. See tussah.

wilton. A multiple-element cut-pile carpet. 47, 93

woof. See filling.

wool. A natural-protein fiber derived from the fleecy undercoats of sheep. 16, 25, 32, 34, 46, 50, 54, 60, 68, 96, 98, 99, 101, 104, 105, 109, 123

woolen system. A spinning process in which short wool fibers are carded and spun into soft, fuzzy, loosely twisted yarn. 50, 54, 60

Wool Mark. A stamp of approval issued by the International Wool Secretariat to denote selected hundred-percent-pure virgin wool. 54, 97

worsted system. A spinning process in which long wool fibers are carded, combed, and spun into a smooth, compact yarn with average to high twist. 54

woven-double fabric. A velvet or plush fabric in which two ground cloths are woven one over the other, with the pile yarns woven up and down between them. 93

Wyzenbeek test. A test for abrasion resistance in upholstery fabrics. 32, 121

yarn. A continuous, often plied strand composed of fibers or filaments and used to form cloth. 8, 10, 16, 21, 22, 24, 25, 26, 30, 32, 33, 34, 40, 43, 46, 47, 50, 52, 56, 61, *63*, 64, 65, 70, 72, 79, 84, 88, 92, 93, 94, 97, 99, 100, 104, 105, 108, 109, 110, 122, 129

yarn dyeing. Dyeing at the yarn stage of the production continuum rather than stock, solution or piece dyeing. 33, 108, 115, 129

yoyo. See hiking.

Zantrel. Trade name of a high-wet-modulus-rayon fiber produced by American Enka.

Zefran. Trade name of an acrylic fiber produced by Dow Badische.

Zefkrome. Trade name of a solution-dyed acrylic fiber produced by Dow Badische.

Ze pel. Trade name of a fluorochemical finish that resists water- and oil-borne stains produced by Du Pont. 35, 98

z-twist, or **openband.** The relatively uncommon counterclockwise direction in which yarn is twisted. 61